T.D. Jakes

T.D. Jakes

America's New Preacher

Shayne Lee

NEW YORK UNIVERSITY PRESS

New York and London

NEW YORK UNIVERSITY PRESS
New York and London
www.nyupress.org

Library of Congress Cataloging-in-Publication Data
Lee, Shayne.
T.D. Jakes : America's new preacher / Shayne Lee.
p. cm.
Includes bibliographical references and index.
ISBN–13: 978–0–8147–5205–0 (alk. paper)
ISBN–10: 0–8147–5205–5 (alk. paper)
1. Jakes, T. D. I. Title.
BX8762.5.Z8J35   2005
289.9'4'092—dc22   2005010578

New York University Press books are printed on acid-free paper,
and their binding materials are chosen for strength and durability.

Manufactured in the United States of America

10 9 8 7 6 5 4 3 2 1

Contents

Preface

In today's religious climate, many pastors run their churches like Fortune 500 corporations vying for market share. Like large conglomerates that make Americans passive victims of ads for pop drinks and sports cars, celebrity preachers use the airways, print media, and cyberspace to inundate Christian consumers with ads for sermon videos, music CDs, and conferences. Televangelists demonstrate that it is now technologically possible to reproduce and market spirituality through a variety of mediums. Accordingly, many spiritual leaders are enjoying the million-dollar homes, flashy wardrobes, and lavish lifestyles derived from transforming their spiritual gifts into salable commodities for mass consumption. No other minister depicts our postmodern age of commercialized spirituality more than Bishop T.D. Jakes.

Time magazine's coverage of Jakes in 2001, asking "Is This Man the Next Billy Graham?" was a watershed event, questioning if a black neo-Pentecostal preacher could be America's next leading religious luminary. It is hard to believe that less than fifteen years ago, Jakes' celebrity barely extended beyond West Virginia coal-mining towns. This country preacher combined talent and tenacity with impeccable timing to help him become one of the most influential spiritual leaders of his generation.

While media moguls like Oprah Winfrey and journalists like David Van Biema tap into Jakes' widespread appeal, academics have been virtually silent about this new American folk hero and his intriguing ministry. Sociologists and religious scholars have been slow to investigate how much Jakes' rapid rise and extraordinary ministry divulge about contemporary religion. Jakes is the signpost of a new age in American Protestantism where spiritual leaders blend compassion with capitalism, pop culture with therapeutic spirituality, and evangelical preaching with pizzazz, style, and organizational savvy. Jakes is profoundly human, self-empowering, pluralistic, high-tech, and multidimensional—a model of the new postmodern evangelical preacher.

Not unlike most powerful men and women, Jakes is a complicated individual brimming with paradoxes and contradictions. There is Jakes the compassionate minister next to Jakes the ferocious self-promoter. There is Jakes the feminist juxtaposed to Jakes the sexist. There is Jakes the liberationist alongside Jakes the conservative capitalist. And there is Jakes the old-fashioned preacher next to Jakes the sensual dramatist. The public response to his complexities is equally ambivalent. Some admire Jakes' frontier spirit and heroic quest toward self-creation and reinvention, while others chastise him for commercializing spirituality.

In the challenging endeavor of writing the first in-depth analysis of a superstar like Jakes, I benefited from the assistance of many people. I am tremendously grateful to Milmon Harrison for his trenchant observations and constructive criticisms on earlier drafts; I cannot imagine how this work would have turned out without his suggestions. I am equally indebted to my brother Travis for his inspiration and input through countless conversations about Jakes and American religion. I must also thank Jennifer Hammer of New York University Press for supporting my work in every way possible; her encouragement and guidance made finishing and revising this book an invaluable learning experience. I thank my parents, Elaine and Ernest, and my sister Dorothy for their wisdom and encouragement, as well as the various family members, friends, and colleagues who endured the constant ramblings about my research. I also owe a debt of thanks to the spiritual leaders and religious scholars who, along with Jakes' staff and church members, peers in ministry, childhood neighbors and friends, conference attendees, and critics, sat through long interviews and provided tremendous insight. Douglas Allen, Brad Braxton, Charlene Burgess, Delores Carpenter, James Cone, David Daniels, James Forbes, Gwen Gomes, Justin Graves, Leonard Lovett, Carlton Pearson, Sarah Jordan Powell, Frederick K.C. Price, Ernestine Reems, Harold Dean Trulear Jr., Vanessa Weatherspoon, Renita Weems, Delores Williams, and Jesse Williams deserve special thanks for their contributions.

T.D. Jakes speaks to his generation, and therefore a book contextualizing his place in the American religious landscape is long overdue. My objective for writing this book is not to celebrate or condemn the man, message, or ministry, but to provide clarity and context to Jakes' rapid rise and far-reaching renown. The pervasive theme of this work demonstrates how the wildfire of his popularity and the flames of his controversy expand from the same accelerator: Thomas Dexter Jakes is an American phenomenon.

T.D. Jakes

Introduction

Imagine tens of thousands of men running up and down the aisles of a large stadium. Many are young, some middle aged, and others in their twilight years. At various points they are jumping, laughing, singing, dancing, and hugging. Now visualize almost twice as many women sitting throughout a large stadium in another city pensively concentrating on every word uttered by the speaker. What do these mental images have in common? Both can be seen at yearly conferences that draw multitudes of people waiting to receive spiritual insights from a tall, husky preacher named Thomas Dexter Jakes.

Few pop stars, let alone spiritual leaders, can attract enough eager spectators to sell out a large stadium, but T.D. Jakes drew 130,000 people to Mega Fest 2004, his three-day family vacation event in Atlanta. Whether he is headlining Reliant Stadium in Houston or the Super Dome in New Orleans, Jakes entices tens of thousands of people to attend his conferences. Moreover, millions of people watch his television broadcasts and purchase his books, videos, and music CDs. For this reason, *Time* magazine distinguished Jakes as "America's preacher" and hinted he may be the next Billy Graham.

Time's association of Jakes with an American icon like Graham punctuates the long way Jakes has come since his humble days preaching in the coal-mining towns of West Virginia. There are conspicuous similarities between Graham and Jakes. Both were sixteen when they made serious commitments to the faith, and both were salesmen before they were preachers. Like Graham,

Jakes began his career relatively unknown and quickly became famous through television and media exposure. Like Graham, Jakes runs a spiritual enterprise with annual budgets in the tens of millions of dollars. Both are featured in major media outlets and have been honored and praised by U.S. presidents. But along with the similarities are stark contrasts.

Jakes, a black neo-Pentecostal, is impacting contemporary popular culture in ways that Graham, a white Evangelical, is not. Unlike Jakes, Graham has never produced a best-selling novel, paperbacks on weight loss and financial prosperity, theatrical productions, and music CDs. Unlike Graham, Jakes draws from pop culture and contextualizes Christianity with contemporary trends in society. Graham's strong suit is preaching a simple yet compelling message of salvation, while Jakes' forte is addressing complex pathologies such as sexual abuse and addictive relationships with a blend of scripture, psychology, and Grandma's folk wisdom.

What Jakes is doing today is not entirely unique in American religion. Historically, popular revivalists like Charles Finney, D.L. Moody, and Arturo Skinner also drew large crowds by preaching electrifying sermons. Today, celebrity preachers like Fred Price, Creflo Dollar, and Benny Hinn also reach millions each year through television broadcasts; clerics like Eddie Long and Bill Hybels also preside over mega churches exceeding 20,000 members; and spiritual leaders like Rick Warren and Joel Osteen also write best-selling books. But Jakes is distinguished by the breadth of his personal talent and the scope of his intellectual reach and business savvy. As the pastor of one of the largest churches in the country, the CEO of a multimillion dollar empire, the host of a television program, the author of a dozen best-sellers, the executive producer of a movie, two Grammy Award nominated music CDs, and three critically acclaimed plays, T.D. Jakes has emerged as one of the most prolific spiritual leaders of our time.

In 2002, in an interview on the popular television program *Best Damn Sports Show Period*, former boxing champion Mike

Tyson declared, "I'm a Muslim, I pray five times a day and even I love T.D. Jakes." Marsha Atkins, a computer analyst and divorced mother of four, claims no man has had more influence on her life than T.D. Jakes. Sociologist Nancy Eiesland believes he is one of the most ingenious spiritual leaders of his era, and the well-known pastor Carlton Pearson considers Jakes to be a prophetic sign and wonder. Sports personality Deion Sanders calls him "Daddy," and millions of people nationwide perceive Jakes as a mouthpiece for God, shepherd to the shattered, and minister of mercy.

Jakes' detractors, however, view him through more carnal lenses as a shyster. They argue that with his exorbitant speaking fees and excessive entrepreneurialism, Jakes turns religion into his most valuable commodity. Rather than representing him as God's comforter, critics portray Jakes as a marketing genius who exploits people's pain, a con artist who tells people what they want to hear—the "Velcro Bishop" with a watered down gospel.

Others are as of yet undecided about the Jakes phenomenon. These individuals may have heard about his numerous best-sellers and wondered how he became so popular. They may have heard Jakes waxing eloquently on *The Oprah Winfrey Show*, National Public Radio, *Larry King Live*, *Charlie Rose*, CSPAN, or the *Tom Joyner Show*, and wondered how he caught America's ear. Like F. Scott Fitzgerald's mysterious fictional character Jay Gatsby, Jakes has curious onlookers scratching their heads at his success and wondering, "How did he pull this off?"

To answer this question, I spent three years systematically studying Jakes and conducting interviews and conversations with his childhood neighbors, longtime friends, church members, peers in ministry, conference attendees. I also spoke with leading scholars of religion and critics of his ministry. In one of my interviews the prominent theologian Delores Williams asked, "So what's your spin?" My retort to her curious inquiry is that my spin is not to produce another celebrity biography, but rather to present Jakes as a prism through which the reader may learn more about contemporary American religion. My thesis is that Jakes generates many followers and critics because he personifies American ideals and postmodern features that resonate with a diversity of psychosocial needs and cultural tastes.

Although American culture has always been about mixing, combining, and recombining elements from a variety of sources, a postmodern shift is causing many people to reevaluate conventional ways of perceiving and classifying the world. This cultural turn is characterized by our nation's growing obsession with image and style, along with a far-reaching pattern of changes in architecture, aesthetics, science, literature, law, entertainment, and other important social and cultural spheres. Our postmodern age is also distinguished by the relentless penetration of advertising, television, and other media into people's lives as well as the fragmented identities and new values that derive from continuous exposure to a saturation of ideas and images. Religion is a great place to see this progression at work, and Jakes' ministry is clearly at the heart of this American dynamism.

Now, Jakes is not postmodern in the same way that intellectuals like the late Jacques Derrida deconstruct truth claims and bask in relativity. Nor is he postmodern in the manner that entertainers like Madonna challenge gender norms with risqué displays of sexuality. But Jakes does share many postmodern traits that are commensurate with contemporary trends in American culture. Jakes saturates the marketplace with an incessant flow of images and products, offers therapeutic religion, and mixes "codes" from assorted elements of contemporary and secular culture. He obscures traditional lines of distinction between the secular and sacred, emphasizes personal experience over doctrinal constraints, and supports denominational independence over church hierarchy. Hence, Jakes is self-empowering, pluralistic, high-tech, and multidimensional—a model of the new postmodern evangelical preacher.

Evangelicals affirm the historicity and reliability of the Bible and represent a large proportion of American Protestants. Until recently, social analysts have failed to understand the diversity that exists among evangelical churches and why some thrive in membership while others decline. Scholars of religion are now realizing attractive features of postmodern evangelical churches in contrast to their traditional counterparts. Donald Miller contended that the popularity of "new-paradigm" churches derives from their ability to convey spirituality in profound and life-changing ways while appropriating stylistic and technological elements from our culture (Miller 1997). Similarly, Kimon Howland Sargeant studied "seeker" congregations that modify programs and services for nonbelievers and attract members by deemphasizing religious symbols and denominational affiliations and by designing worship services according to secular music and style (Sargeant 2000). Both Miller and Sargeant explored a growth spurt of predominantly white churches that are packaging spirituality in a postmodern style while maintaining conservative theology.

African Americans embody the same trends and features found in popular white Protestant movements but often fail to receive the same level of attention until a superstar like Jakes materializes. In this way Jakes symbolizes a new and thriving congregational model that has emerged in the last few decades—one I have coined "the new black church." What distinguishes Jakes and the new black church is their ability to combine an otherworldly experience of ecstatic worship and spiritual enlightenment with a this-worldly emphasis on style, image, and economic prosperity. The genius of the new black church is the flexibility, sophistication, and ingenuity to use twenty-first-century technology to win twenty-first-century souls. What separates the new black church from traditional churches is the savvy and willingness to contextualize Christianity for contemporary needs and culture, while not compromising a vigorous support for biblical authority. What differentiates Jakes and leaders of the new black church is a keen understanding of postmodern culture and an inexorable drive to produce spiritual commodities for mass consumption in an ever-expanding market.

But more than a symbol of the new black church, Jakes is the signpost for postdenominational Protestant America in general. Jakes' success indicates a religious realignment in our nation that causes many mainline churches that are stuck in tradition to decline while innovative independent churches experience phenomenal growth. In today's religious landscape, the degree to which churches and preachers thrive depends upon their ability to package and market spirituality to meet the relevant needs and tastes of Americans. Denominational loyalty is becoming a thing of the past as more baby boomers and Gen X-ers are seeking new forms of spirituality that appeal to them rather than blindly accepting familial traditions or affiliations (McRoberts 2003; Wuthnow 1988). Preachers like Jakes are drawing many followers by delivering therapeutic and transformative messages while providing spiritual commodities that are more in tune with postmodern sensibilities. But they are also drawing critics who feel that matching Christianity with the existential cravings of contemporary Americans compromises the gospel of Christ.

Jakes is a construction in the backdrop of larger cultural and structural changes that prepared the ground for his amazing rise. This book emphasizes the "Americanness" of his story and delineates the new movements, commercial networks, and innovative uses of media and marketing techniques that together make up a kind of "faith industry" out of which Jakes and other popular preachers are able to emerge with a peculiar kind of market niche and fame. I demonstrate how new technologies and cultural changes are affecting religious exchanges and how Jakes' success occurred in our new media age of hype and simulation that churns out celebrities almost overnight. Hence, like tennis player and model Anna Kournikova and basketball star LeBron James, Jakes is an American phenomenon.

As a man of his times and the embodiment of values and tensions of his era, Jakes shares striking similarities with another archetypal American, the classic fictional character Jay Gatsby. Both Jakes and Gatsby came from humble beginnings and used hard work and discipline early in their youth to embark on the process of self-creation. Both traveled far distances across the American frontier in quest of financial fulfillment, and both became legendary figures and fabulously wealthy. Both are the products of historical moments and opportunity structures that brought their individual initiative to bear, and yet both represent all that is good about America's penchant for improvisation and transcendence.

However, Gatsby and Jakes are complex figures who also personify a darker side of America. Gatsby's story is a commentary on the greed and corruption of the Jazz Age, and Jakes' story epitomizes troubling aspects of our postmodern age where some fear that religion may be degenerating into just another business enterprise. Like Gatsby, Jakes yields to the material seductions of consumer culture, and his blend of religion and capitalism rouses many doubts about our nation's spiritual direction. Some feel Jakes' brand of Christianity is too commercial, too trendy, too self-indulgent, and, hence, too American.

In a nutshell, this book is about a pastor with a passionate desire to heal the brokenhearted and a shrewd entrepreneur with a pit-bull tenacity for protecting and expanding his empire. It is about religious innovation, postmodern spirituality, and commercialized Christianity. It is an epic of self-invention with Jakes' life, message, and ministry as windows through which we can see a clearer vision of contemporary religion and America. Hence, to understand America is to understand Jakes, and to understand Jakes we begin with his humble beginnings.

[1]

Humble Beginnings

I have lived on both sides of the track, and my shoes have
walked down shanty-town streets and sidewalks paved with
gold. I know that hard work and determination can overcome humble beginnings.   —T.D. Jakes

Rising to the top of any institutional structure generally involves
navigating through a series of predictable junctures on the way. For
example, one sees Harvard, Stanford, Duke, and Kellogg and
Wharton business schools as recurring alma maters on the résumés
of senior executives in Fortune 500 companies. Similarly, prestigious law firms scout for graduates from prominent universities,
and universities like to hire Ivy League graduates. Whether competing as a professional athlete, playing for a Philharmonic, dancing for
Alvin Ailey, becoming a United States senator, or rising up the cler-
ical ranks, most positions of great privilege involve passing through
a number of conventional steps before one can reach the top.

But every once in a while, chance and talent produce improvisational greats like computer moguls Michael Dell and Steve Jobs
or music stars Jewel and Eminem who defy conventional routes
by crafting their own blueprints for success. Now and again, an
elite scholar like Aldon Morris begins his academic career as a student in a community college. Not often, a parent like Richard
Williams raises two daughters, Venus and Serena, outside of the
contours of privileged tennis networks to dominate the game.

And on rare occasions, a country preacher like Thomas Dexter Jakes rises from humble beginnings to become a dominant figure in American Protestantism.

Jakes' ascent veered from the conventional course followed by contemporaries such as Charles Blake, a popular African American pastor of a large church in California. Blake is the son of a prominent pastor, while Jakes is the son of a janitor. Blake was part of a sophisticated religious structure that provided blueprints for success, while Jakes navigated through obscure Pentecostal networks in West Virginia. Thus, Blake followed a predictable path while Jakes had to evolve under the radar; and when Charles Blake surfaced as a prominent spiritual leader, few were surprised; but when T.D. Jakes emerged on the national scene, everyone wondered from where he came. Jakes' lack of strategic networks provided room for the self-invention that contributes to his mass appeal. Like the vagaries of inner-city life developed the toughness and indomitable spirit in Venus and Serena Williams that would one day help them take over the tennis circuit, young Tommy Jakes' early life experiences brought forth the American traits that would later propel him to prominence.

Vandalia and Childhood Complexities

Jakes grew up on Vandalia Hill, a working class community in Charleston, West Virginia, situated on top of a mountain overlooking the city. The Vandalia that young Tommy Jakes knew was the type of mythic neighborhood where residents took responsibility for all the children in the community. It was the kind of environment where everyone knew everyone else and made frequent visits to one another's homes, especially during the holidays. If there was a funeral, people from all over brought food and made sure that the bereaved were supported with love and concern. As one former resident recalled, "We prayed together, we laughed together, we cried together."

Vandalia was a homey kind of town where people addressed each other with playful nicknames. Jakes' brother Ernest was "June," his neighbor Mary Booker was "Pudgy" and her daughter was "Libby," his longtime friend Wes Womack was "Booby," Martha Saunders was "Sweatpea," James Mosely Jr. was "Bimp," Jakes' ace Carol Boddie was "Cuzzie," and Jakes himself was known to many as "Tommy from the Hill." Although Vandalia was racially mixed, blacks and whites lived in separate sections, and Jakes lived in the heart of the black section. Most residents suggested that Vandalia had some racial problems, but for the most part blacks and whites interacted peacefully. The schools were integrated, but the churches were not, and for most black residents, "everything pretty much evolved around the church," according to Libby Booker.

Jakes and some of his friends and neighbors offer different snapshots of his childhood. One area involves his self-confidence. On several occasions Jakes has recalled his early struggles with a lisp and his lack of confidence because of his weight. On the other hand, he impressed his family and friends as an alert four-year-old who could recite all the words to James Weldon Johnson's classic anthem, "Lift Every Voice and Sing." His childhood buddy Bimp described Tommy as confident and articulate with much to say. Jackie Bruer offered that most people in Vandalia knew there was something very special about him, and Jakes' neighbor Eleanor Hacker remembered him as an outspoken boy who was unafraid to talk to adults and strangers.

Jakes and others often give the impression that he did not have much of a childhood and that circumstances forced him to grow up quickly. As Jakes once stated in *Ebony* magazine, "I grew up in an adult world. I had never ridden a bicycle. I was forced to be responsible and deal with issues that relate to life and death" (Starling 2001). Libby Booker noted, "Tommy was kind of an old soul, always focused, always motivated," and another peer added, "I never remember Tommy being involved in Boy Scouts and all that stuff." One family friend suggested that Tommy may have been more comfortable around adults than children his own age.

Jakes and his friends, however, paint a picture of a less somber Tommy full of energy and mischief. Paul Lewis, a longtime friend of Jakes, claimed, "We had a normal childhood; we were just kids and we got into lots of stuff." Paul lived four blocks from Jakes and everyday they trekked through the woods together to make their one-mile journey to elementary school. Paul reminisced about Tommy charming the cafeteria lady to give him extra portions of macaroni and cheese, and he revealed a legendary incident in junior high school when Tommy, in a fit of anger, lifted up his small gym teacher and placed him on a coat hook. Mary Booker remembers Tommy frequently coming over to her house to play with her daughter Libby and two sons, Jeff and Jim. Tina Dean, one of Jakes' closest childhood friends, added that Tommy was ingenuous and did not wait for fun to come to him. Tommy and Tina enjoyed hiking through the woods and cooking together.

Tommy spent many carefree childhood summers south of Charleston visiting his aunt, who supplied him with fresh pecans from her yard. On many occasions, Tommy and his siblings entertained one another by performing talent shows for their parents. Bobbie Tolliver, Jakes' next-door neighbor and longtime family friend, remembers Tommy as a brilliant and fun kid with a lot of questions and even more mischief. Tommy and Tolliver's son, Wyatt Jr., were responsible for many rascally acts in the neighborhood. Tommy had a good sense of humor and was known for his many childhood pranks on family friends. He lived with Bobbie Tolliver for a month while his parents visited Ohio for medical treatment, and she received many calls from school reporting his roguish antics. Although Tolliver has fond memories of hearing young Tommy preaching from his living room, she admitted to being surprised by his decision to enter the ministry because she thought he would be a businessman.

Libby Booker remembered him as a cordial friend whom everyone loved, while a former neighbor recalled a more petulant Tommy who would sass adult neighbors and intimidate his peers. Jakes recently admitted that he was spoiled because, "After all, I was the baby of the family and I usually ended up getting what I wanted" (Jakes 2003b:35). Tommy gave his mother some gray hairs. As a first-grader, he "borrowed" his mother's diamond ring and gave it to Elvira, the girl down the street, as a token of his love, for which he received a rare spanking from his mother upon its return. Tommy once violated his mother's curfew by stuffing pillows under his covers and sneaking out of the house, only to be filled with guilt the next morning for disobeying and deceiving her. Tommy's tremendous guilt and reflection after violating his mother's trust demonstrated his early desire to walk the straight and narrow.

On occasion, Tommy and Tina would skip school and go to Tina's house to cook meals. Tina claims Jakes still makes the best upside-down pineapple cake she has ever eaten. Sometimes Tommy excelled in the classroom, other times he was in trouble, and as Jakes put it, "One day it seemed I was destined for success, and the next my mother would wonder how I would end up" (Jakes 2000:88). Overall, he was a bright young kid with good days and bad, triumphs and trials, visible talents, secret struggles, and low self-esteem. Most agreed with Libby Booker's statement that "Tommy had the discipline and focus early enough in life to fulfill his destiny."

In his books and sermons, Jakes also provides a complicated portrayal of his family's socioeconomic status during his youth. He paints a picture of early financial struggle, exemplified by his embarrassment in bringing his lunch to school in a greasy brown paper bag because his parents could not afford the fancy Snoopy or Mickey Mouse lunchboxes carried by many of his peers. In his book *Maximize the Moment*, Jakes recalled his family's long Sunday drives as the only amusement they could afford. Jakes' older sister, Jacqueline, mused that "Momma had a knack for budgeting and she stretched her grocery money by fixing us affordable and nutritious food" (J. Jakes 2002:181).

Contrary to these accounts, Jakes often depicts his mother running small businesses and his father as a man who transcended poverty to reach considerable success. Libby Booker mentioned Jakes' family as one of the first to own a brick house, and Jakes often discusses how his father turned a one-man cleaning operation into a janitorial business with fifty-two employees, three offices, and ten trucks. It is difficult to assess how the janitorial empire is juxtaposed with the long car rides in the rusty 1957 Chevy and the greasy brown paper bags in place of lunch boxes—all happening before Tommy's tenth birthday, when Ernest Sr.'s business began to dissolve after he suffered a debilitating illness.

Tenacity and Entrepreneurial Spirit

"Those Jakeses were some selling fools," exclaimed one former neighbor in jest. Vandalia was the type of community where "people worked hard for what they had and most owned their own homes and did everything possible to make ends meet," according to Eleanor Hacker. It was usual for parents to have a couple of jobs, and Ernest Sr. spent almost every waking hour working, as his daughter Jacqueline confirmed in her book (J. Jakes 2002:133). In addition to janitorial duties at local grocery stores and at the West Virginia capitol building, Ernest Sr. sold all sorts of things from the back of his green truck, including fish and frog legs. His wife, Odith, a grade-school teacher, sold Avon products in her spare time. Tommy helped his parents with their endeavors and established his own entrepreneurial agenda cutting grass and selling vegetables.

Ernest Sr. contributed to his son's entrepreneurial drive, but Jakes attributes his faith and tenacity to his mother. Though Jakes has fond memories of the playful hand of his father brushing his forehead and telling him stories, Ernest Sr. worked so many hours that Odith practically raised her three children alone, teaching them how to cook, sew, and clean. Odith learned persistence and hard work from her mother, who took in laundry from neighbors to finance her return to college at the age of fifty and embarked on a new career as a schoolteacher. Tommy's grandmother passed her grit and discipline to Odith, who entered Tuskegee when she was fifteen and completed her degree when she was eighteen.

Odith created an atmosphere in the home where self-actualization was inevitable for her children. She taught Jacqueline, Ernest Jr., and Tommy to express themselves freely, and she motivated them toward excellence in all of their endeavors, as she discussed in the foreword of one of Jakes' books:

> I taught them to shoot for the top. I taught them to be all they could be. I remember telling them, "If you become a street sweeper, be the best one on the road. If you become a teacher, be the best one in the school." (Jakes 1996c:xi)

Tommy hung around his mother when she keynoted luncheons and banquets for her sorority. After one particular speaking engagement, the precocious six-year-old was prescient: "Today, I travel with you and listen while you speak, but the time will come when you will travel with me and I will speak" (Jakes 1994b:26). Odith played an integral role in fastening Tommy's entrepreneurial initiative by driving through snow to help him deliver newspapers.

To understand Jakes' current business enterprises, we must look back to the pesky entrepreneurialism in his youth. Tommy emulated his parents' sense of industry as an eight-year-old, selling vegetables from his mother's garden. His neighbor Bobbie Tolliver remembered that little Tommy strolling down the street with bags of vegetables in each hand was a common sight in Vandalia. During the harvest season he was out hustling every day, and the weight of dragging those heavy bags up and down West Virginia's hills often hurt his back. Those bags of greens were early lessons that taught him how to press toward his goal with relentlessness stronger than the rudeness he sometimes faced from neighbors when offering his wares. Whether he was cutting his neighbor Minerva Coles' grass, rising early every morning to deliver newspapers, or selling Avon cosmetics and Amway products throughout high school, Jakes showed early flashes of the doggedness that would later help him become a business mogul. His industrious family legacy and early life experiences bestowed upon him the talent and tenacity he would later use to turn his message and ministry into a multimillion dollar empire.

Family Tragedy

Young Tommy's entrepreneurial activity came to an abrupt pause when his father was diagnosed with a debilitating kidney disease. Ernest Sr.'s chronic kidney ailment necessitated dialysis to remove waste and excess liquid from his blood. Almost daily, Tommy and siblings watched their father's blood being transported through tubes to a dialyzer that cleaned and transported the blood back to his body. Tommy played his part by mopping up blood from around the dialysis machine. This experience had a profound impact on Tommy's psyche.

Jakes rarely discusses how he felt watching his three-hundred-pound father deteriorate into "a little wisp of a man," as a neighbor described him. Jakes seldom mentions the numerous hospital visits and the times he cried himself to sleep. He never publicly discusses his parents' separation and divorce, which stemmed from the vicissitudes of Ernest Sr.'s fight for his life. But handling his father's ailment did not quench Tommy's entrepreneurial drive. While his peers were dating and enjoying their first years in high school, Tommy was aggressively selling Avon products in tandem with picking up the pieces of his tattered family life.

Tommy's experience of caring for his invalid father helped him to mature quickly and become a sympathetic teenager. He spent many days and nights in a hospital with other kids and parents dying around him, learning to convey compassion at an early age. Jakes now admits that his father's illness had everything to do with instilling in him the sensitivity and uncanny ability to speak to people's pain, a talent that would differentiate his future ministry as shepherd to the shattered.

In 1972, Ernest Jakes Sr. passed away at the young age of forty-eight after a six-year battle with kidney disease. His death taught Tommy that the gulf between living and dying was shorter than most realized and that he must make good use of every moment while alive. This truism of maximizing each moment would later serve as an integral theme in Jakes' ministry. Ernest Sr.'s death also intensified Tommy's Christian commitment and inspired him to find solace in the church.

Grace and Power

Many of Tommy's spiritual discoveries occurred when he was alone. Ernest Sr. had a Methodist background, Odith was Baptist, and neither was particularly dogmatic during the early development of their children. Though Tommy's parents taught moral scruples, principles of healthy living, and a strong faith in God, they were not religious in the sense of being active in the church and creating a spiritual environment in the home. This provided Tommy much room to carve out his own spiritual path.

Tommy first attended First Baptist Church of Vandalia, "a little Baptist church in the hills of West Virginia on the side of a mountain in prayer meetings with little old ladies who sang old songs that you don't remember anymore," as he later recalled at AZUSA 2000, a conference in Tulsa, Oklahoma. Tommy's peers gave him the moniker "Bible Boy" because he carried a Bible during many of his travels. Like many impressionable young products of the black church experience, young Tommy made his backyard his cathedral and squirrels his early congregants. He preached his first sermons in the wind, and his spirit and fervor were often heard by neighbors.

Tommy exemplified an interest in spirituality at a young age. While other kids were playing in the Vandalia Recreational Center, Eleanor Hacker remembers Tommy making frequent visits to her home to read scriptures with her father, Robert Hutchinson. As a teenager, Tommy was into music and exhibited leadership skills as the director of a choir consisting of eight or nine of his peers. When Tommy took over the choir he made the music more contemporary, demonstrating his early fondness for innovation. He played the piano, sang, and was a hard taskmaster with tremendous dedication and focus.

The early years at First Baptist Church of Vandalia introduced Tommy to an emphasis on God's grace and a respect for human frailties—principles he still holds dearly—but there was a craving in his young heart to experience what he later described as "the fullness of the Holy Spirit." One night as a teenager, Tommy accompanied his choir to sing at a small Pentecostal church called Greater Emanuel Gospel Tabernacle. As Jakes recalled, Greater Emanuel was filled with large black women wearing white dresses, prayer caps, and no makeup. During the service, Tommy realized they were emphasizing the presence of the Holy Spirit and he cried out saying, "Lord, if it is real then let it happen to me," and then he began speaking in tongues, a manifestation that Pentecostals teach is the evidence of a new spiritual experience of God's power.

Although he came back periodically to help out with the music, Tommy left First Baptist Church of Vandalia to join Greater Emanuel in 1972. In contrast to the emphasis on God's grace and human frailty he learned at First Baptist, Tommy quickly became acclimated to the Pentecostal experience of church mothers calling on the name of Jesus, and preachers offering sermons such as "Get Right or Get Out!" and "Holiness or Hell." Norman Jones, then a deacon at Greater Emanuel, described those early days when Tommy joined:

It was a tongue-talking, fire baptized church that we lived in holiness and holiness was a way of living. It seemed like everybody was on fire for the Lord. It was a church that had a lot of energy and songs and dance and it was an exhibit of lifestyle going out to help other people. (Interview)

Tommy's initial years at Greater Emanuel involved intense struggles with depression and feelings of inadequacy because he was a teenager surrounded by devout Pentecostal Christians who rarely showed vulnerability. This left him questioning his own imperfection:

I was young and so impressionable. Secretly suffering from low self-esteem, I thought that the Christians around me had mastered a level of holiness that seemed to evade me. I groaned in the night; I cried out to God to create in me a robot-like piety that would satisfy what I thought was required of me. (Jakes 2001:89)

This was a difficult time for him because none of the believers at his church shared with him that they had also experienced battles before they obtained victories. Much stress and guilt also came from the fact that Tommy, a heavy smoker since elementary school, was now attending a church with pious Pentecostals who viewed cigarette smoking as a sin against the body, which the Bible teaches is God's temple. Tommy soon became weary of using breath mints and spraying himself down with air freshener before coming to church to avoid the condemnation of his fellow worshipers. His relief finally came in a Watch Night Service when he fell on his knees and cried out to God for deliverance. He never smoked another cigarette.

Tommy's early battles in a community of "invulnerable" saints left an indelible mark on his life and future ministry because those inner conflicts fashioned a disdain for self-righteousness in the church. Like Protestant reformer Martin Luther, Tommy grew to believe that God's power does not negate human frailty and that

God's merit comes only through faith in Christ rather than works of righteousness. His personal battles birthed in him a healthy respect for the human condition and prepared him for a future ministry as an iconoclast fighting what he saw as Christian hypocrisy.

Tommy at sixteen years of age could have been preparing for the SAT, but the demands of the moment imposed their will on his future and limited his scholastic achievements. He spent part of his high school experience overwhelmed by his father's death and the other part as the recipient of brutal mocking because of his growing faith. According to Paul Lewis, their peers ridiculed Tommy for trying to be a Christian. Consequently, Tommy dropped out of high school and accepted the call to preach. His early years in ministry included trials, tragedies, and humble beginnings.

Jakes' early ministry training was in an association of churches called Greater Emanuel International Fellowship. While large Pentecostal denominations like the Church of God in Christ and the Assemblies of God were joining the ranks among the Protestant mainstream in the 1970s, Greater Emanuel International Fellowship remained an obscure network of small Pentecostal churches with fiery but relatively unknown preachers. Accordingly, much of Jakes' early preaching experiences were in storefronts. Jakes also endured struggles with abject poverty, depression, and family tragedies while he preached throughout West Virginia's coal-mining towns. For Jakes to emerge out of such a landscape is a testimony to his early capacity for transcendence.

Pentecostals and Apostolics

Scholars commonly regard the Azusa Street Revival of 1906 as the beginning of the modern Pentecostal movement. This spiritual revival included three years of pulsating services with white and black Christians worshiping together in a dilapidated warehouse on Azusa Street in Los Angeles. The revival's spiritual energy, excitement, and novel beliefs about the baptism of the Holy Spirit sparked the development of new churches and networks as part of what proponents quickly identified as the Pentecostal movement. Religion scholar Harvey Cox's book *Fire from Heaven* brought even more attention to the fact that Pentecostalism was the fastest-growing Christian movement of the twentieth century.

The Pentecostal movement introduced new theological presuppositions about the Holy Spirit's role in the life of the believer, strict moral codes, and an emphasis on eschewing worldly pleasures. The dominant doctrinal themes of the early Pentecostal movement were the imminent return of Jesus and the practice of speaking in tongues, a practice the New Testament book of Acts mentions as a gift the Holy Spirit bestows on believers to communicate in an unlearned language. Distinguishing themselves from mainline Protestants who claimed there is only one baptism at salvation, Pentecostals argued that the practice of speaking in tongues signifies that one has received a second baptism of spiritual empowerment. Pentecostals also placed greater emphasis on Christians' ability to engage in supernatural activity such as healing, prophesying, and casting out demons, whereas Baptists and other Protestants were restrained or cautious concerning the spiritual gifts mentioned in the New Testament. From the new movement's inception, the Pentecostal practice of speaking in tongues became a source of contention with mainline Protestants. Extreme practices such as snake and fire handling were mainly limited to Pentecostals in the most culturally detached regions of the Ozarks and the lower Appalachians (Anderson 1979).

Like most American Protestant movements, the Pentecostal movement was integrated before succumbing to the segregated racial patterns of America. The first official Pentecostal denomination, the Church of God in Christ (COGIC), led by a black preacher named Charles Harrison Mason, was interracial between 1907 and 1914 and played a unique role by ordaining hundreds of black and white ministers of independent congregations from 1907 to 1914. Inspired by a growing desire for social distance, disgruntled white ministers from COGIC began to meet around 1911 to discuss putting together their own denomination, which eventually led to the formation of the Assemblies of God. The Assemblies of God quickly became the largest and most centralized entity of white Pentecostal Christians and paved the way for a segregated Pentecostal movement.

By the Second World War, the growth of Pentecostalism had spread rapidly and was organized along racial lines in segregated denominations. Most white Pentecostals became affiliated with the Assemblies of God or smaller denominations like the Pentecostal Holiness Church, the Church of God, the Four Square Church, and the United Pentecostal Church. Black Pentecostals remained with COGIC and with smaller black denominations like the United Pentecostal Council of the Assemblies of God, the United Holy Church; some participated in the plurality of Apostolic movements such as the Pentecostal Assemblies of the World. Though once marginalized, by the 1970s, Pentecostalism grew in power and influence, and the Assemblies of God and COGIC became part of the religious mainstream, but smaller Apostolic Pentecostal networks remained on the fringes of American Protestantism.

Apostolic churches represent a small branch of Pentecostals distinguished by their rejection of a Trinitarian perspective of God. Pentecostals, like most Protestants, traditionally believe in the Trinity—one God but three distinct persons: the Father, the Son, and the Holy Spirit—whereas Apostolic Christians believe that the Godhead is only in the person of Jesus Christ and hence they call themselves Oneness Pentecostals. Apostolics are adamant about Christians being baptized in the name of Jesus, rather than in the name of the Father, Son, and Holy Spirit like most Protestants. Though on the surface this may seem like a minor difference, it reflects the Apostolics' emphatic rejection of any ritual that alludes to a Trinitarian Godhead rather than the Oneness perspective. Many Protestants believe Oneness doctrine to be heretical.

In spite of these important differences, Thomas Jakes' first visit to an Apostolic church in West Virginia introduced him to a world not much different from more mainstream Pentecostal churches of the day. Like most Pentecostals, Apostolics speak in tongues and teach that the power of God is available to all believers. And like most traditional Pentecostal churches, Apostolic churches are generally sectarian in nature and shun "worldly" pleasures like watching movies and dancing to secular music, while emphasizing the necessity of living a sanctified or holy life.

When Jakes joined Greater Emanuel Gospel Tabernacle as a teenager, he began what would become a lifelong affiliation with Apostolic denominations and associations. Greater Emanuel Gospel Tabernacle was part of a network of churches in the Ohio and West Virginia area called Greater Emanuel Apostolic Faith Tabernacle, which later changed its name to Greater Emanuel International Fellowship. Jakes' early mentors came from this network, including Bishop Curtis Lindsey, who was pastor at Greater Emanuel Gospel Tabernacle when Jakes attended, and Bishop Sherman Watkins, an influential preacher from Ohio who took an early liking to Jakes and fathered him in the ministry.

Jakes was a regional bishop for Greater Emanuel International Fellowship early in his career until Watkins started a new Apostolic fellowship in 1988 called the Higher Ground Always Abounding Assemblies, which Jakes joined and where he still remains a high-ranking bishop. Lindsey and Watkins were instrumental in his progress but lacked the power, institutional contacts, and national visibility wielded by the clergy of larger black denominations so they can navigate young preaching prodigies like Jakes to prominence. Additionally, Jakes began his preaching career in an obscure West Virginia locality without the backing of a family name in ministry.

Early Preaching Days

After accepting the call to ministry at age seventeen, Jakes preached his first sermon two years later. He was nervous and his hands would shake so badly that he could barely use a microphone. He also began preaching with a great fear of scrutiny, dread of not living up to people's expectations, wrestling with feelings of unworthiness. But once he overcame his fear of public speaking and the insecurities about his lisp, it was obvious to onlookers that he would eventually become a great preacher. Norman Jones, then a deacon in his church, discussed how Jakes demonstrated a mysterious ability to breathe life into biblical texts with colorful illustrations and an expansive array of scriptures at his disposal.

In his late teens, Jakes returned to First Baptist Church of Vandalia as part-time musical director while still exploring his new Pentecostal environs at Greater Emanuel Gospel Tabernacle. After finishing his high school equivalency requirements, Jakes briefly attended West Virginia State College but had to quit after a year because his job at a chemical plant demanded more of his time. Odith Jakes' graduate studies in psychology more than likely influenced her son's decision to major in the same subject during his brief stint in college. The fact that Jakes never completed his degree is inconsequential, but what is important concerns his decision to major in psychology: it provided him with a framework for healing the mind that became an important feature of his ministry. His early psych classes inspired Jakes to address the existential concerns and emotional traumas of the human condition.

In a place like West Virginia where jobs are scarce, many young men are relegated to the dangerous task of mining the mountains for sulfur coal reserves. Jakes, however, worked at the Linde Division of Union Carbine, a chemical plant in Charleston, and maintained a hectic schedule as a part-time preacher and musical director. Jakes was quite fortunate to work at the chemical plant, which provided the opportunity to live in relative comfort, as evidenced by the late-model silver Trans Am he purchased to transport him to the mounting speaking engagements, including weddings and funerals. Jakes also worked other odd jobs intermittently, including as assistant manager for a local paint store and as a delivery-truck driver.

Jakes continued to preach in garages, storefronts, and small churches up and down the coal-mining towns that would have him. Around old coal stoves in small churches and empty pews is where Jakes honed his preaching gifts by ministering until he was sweaty and tired. Traveling evangelists often lodged with the pastor and his family in a guest room or in the bed of one of the pastor's children. In a recent series of sermons he called "You Don't Have to Believe in My Dream," Jakes alluded to these humble days of preaching engagements in the West Virginia hills:

> I mean just preaching with no place to change, had to go downstairs in the back to the bathroom, down in the dark and step down in a little dark place and couldn't even see. Weeks of revival, laying on the floor casting out devils, no name, no reputation, no career, nothing like that, getting in the car wet, going home wet, couldn't even change my clothes.

It was normal for him to travel many miles to preach to a handful of destitute people in the backwoods.

The late 1970s to the early 1990s were bittersweet years for Jakes. On the one hand, they brought forth some of the greatest moments of his life, including meeting and marrying Serita, the love of his life. When looking at Serita today, draped in her fancy clothes and expensive jewelry, it is difficult to picture the unadorned coal miner's daughter who met Jakes shortly after he started his first church in Montgomery in 1979. Serita's transformation is a Cinderella story itself because, like Jakes, in her early years she struggled with her weight and low self-esteem. She was tormented by peers who chanted, "Fatty, fatty, two-by-four!" to mock her chubby stature. She also suffered misfortune, including the murder of her older brother and rejection from a violent boyfriend who left her feeling unwanted and reviled. After going off to college, Serita connected with the wrong crowd and experimented with drugs, alcohol, and sex, but due to her mother's perseverance, she eventually straightened up and became a Christian as a young adult.

Serita began to admire this young traveling preacher and sent him secret pen pal letters. She finally had the opportunity to meet her portly prince when her pastor introduced them after Jakes preached at her church, as she discussed in her book:

> My hero stared at me with eyes that I knew would melt me into the carpet. As I approached him, he began to smile that smile. To me he said, "Do you know where a bachelor can get a home-cooked meal?" (S. Jakes 1999:186)

The two began to date for about six months and were married in 1981, two years after Jakes founded the Montgomery storefront with only ten members. Jakes saw in Serita a woman who would walk through hell and high water to support him. Serita foresaw in Jakes a man who was destined for greatness. Both should be credited for discernment because Jakes eventually reached prominence and Serita was an incredible bulwark of support during the difficult days that preceded success. The 1980s and early 1990s were also special because Serita gave birth to four of their five children.

Besides the triumphs, this period also brought some of the most taxing times in terms of Jakes' marriage, ministry, and personal faith. Jakes preached to many empty chairs at the Montgomery storefront church and supplemented his income by continuing to work at the chemical plant. For music, the church used the same mahogany piano his mother bought him for Christmas as an adolescent. The church's finances were so strapped that Jakes had to beg State Electric Supply Company for lightbulbs.

Jakes' young marriage withstood critical moments of pain and suffering during this period, including a death-defying car wreck. The impact of the crash was so great that Jakes' head cracked the windshield. With blood seeping down his face, Jakes banged against the driver's side door, urging his ailing wife to get out of the car, but Serita whispered to him that she could not move. Injuries from the accident immobilized Serita for over a year, and doctors feared that she would never walk again. Through a painstakingly slow rehabilitation process, Serita's foot convalesced and eventually she was able to walk again without crutches. Meanwhile, financial difficulties mounted when the Linde Division at Union Carbine closed down in 1982, leaving Jakes and hundreds of hardworking West Virginians unemployed.

After the plant closed, Jakes endured difficult periods of poverty that included times without electricity or running water. On one occasion when his twin boys were asking why they had the lights off, Jakes consoled them by explaining they were playing hide-and-seek. Jakes' car was repossessed because he could no longer afford payments, and he ended up driving an old rusty Valiant that the embarrassed deacons hid in the back when guests visited the church. When the old car broke down on one occasion, Jakes took the bus to the utility company to beg them to keep his lights on. The company refused, as Jakes recalled:

> I walked out of the utility office and burst into tears. I don't mean the quiet leaking of the tear ducts, either. I mean a deluge of sobbing, heaving, quaking, and wailing. I looked like an insane person walking down the street. (Jakes 1994b:21)

Losing the job at the chemical plant meant that he had to find other means of providing for his wife and toddling twins, including backbreaking work digging ditches to make gas lines. This work produced money for Pampers and groceries, as well as bloody hands and sore feet from long hours of grueling work. Serita mended Jakes' hemorrhaging hands after working in the ditches and lifted his bruised ego after purchasing milk for his young children through the WIC program. There were times when Jakes had to hitch a ride to get back home from preaching engagements, and at one point he and Serita had to trade in pop bottles to buy some baloney for his family. In a recent sermon Jakes humorously alleged that his twins suffer from flashbacks at the very sight of baloney. Jakes often thought he was too young to have to deal with so much and feared the struggles would never end. He was terrified of spending the rest of his life stuck between floors in an intermediate stage of transition.

Serita did not complain when their gas was turned off but showed incredible resilience by waking up early each morning to boil water on an electric range so her family would have hot water to bathe. She never grumbled when she had to collect bottles and work nights in a radio station to earn extra money, or when she had to create new meals out of yesterday's scraps during the bouts on welfare. Serita did not gripe when she had to borrow clothes to attend their denomination's annual meeting, nor when the hems kept falling out of her dresses and her shoes turned over on her feet. She never tired in helping her husband counsel members, conduct worship services, and clean the small Montgomery church. Serita never gave up faith in her husband, his business ideas, preaching gifts, and destiny toward greatness, and she stood by Jakes even when his own faith in God was on trial. Sometimes it did not look like the young family was going to make it out of poverty, but their struggle provided the battle scars that would later help Jakes encourage millions of people in similar hopeless situations.

Jakes Ventures Out

While suffering financially, Jakes was pursuing his ministry with the same tenacity and persistence that helped his father turn mopping a floor into an art form. His storefront church in Montgomery had moderate growth. In 1982 Jakes began to broadcast locally over the radio, and in the following year he held his first conference, which almost eighty people attended. At the time it cost only forty-five dollars for a thirty-minute radio show but the church could barely afford the small price. Jakes continued to work hard and expanded his ministry in whatever way was available to him. When he was not digging ditches and tending to his small church, he was preaching at storefront churches and small revivals in coal-mining towns; at times he received twenty-five-dollar honorariums, and at times he received nothing for his services.

Jakes began exploring strategic opportunities to expand his ministry, which included relocating his Montgomery storefront to a coal-mining city called Smithers when he was in his mid-twenties. What others perceived to be a condemned old movie theater that had been uninhabited for decades, Jakes saw as the perfect building for his church:

> I will never forget the first time I brought our little congregation over to see this miracle of a building. I was shocked when we opened the door and they looked totally disgusted. I couldn't understand why they weren't excited. One of the congregants literally threw up and had to leave because the smell was so bad. (Jakes 2000:141)

The loan his church received was inadequate for the type of work that needed to be done, so Jakes labored long hours to make the building inhabitable. He put his body through abusive bouts of physical sacrifice, during a time when his electricity at home was off. The Jakeses eventually converted the old dilapidated theater into their new house of worship and tears of joy fell down Serita's face when her husband cut the ribbon to dedicate the new church.

Smithers demonstrated to Jakes that his vision could be brought into fruition with the same ingenuity and persistence with which he peddled vegetables to neighbors in his youth. After five years in the town, Jakes relocated the church to 7th Avenue in South Charleston in 1990, and the small church quickly doubled in membership. Jakes and many of his flock lived in South Charleston, so the move was strategic for both growth and convenience. Only a few years later, as he continued to increase in popularity, Jakes relocated the church to a more affluent, predominantly white suburb called Cross Lanes. It is unusual for a pastor to relocate his church three times in his career, let alone in a brief span of only twelve years, but Jakes was not an ordinary pastor. He was making strategic decisions and taking incredible risks to expand his ministry. Each move was a step up because Jakes was willing to do everything possible to further his ministry and influence.

During this twelve-year period of financial struggle, intense traveling, hard work, and church displacements, Jakes was also forming relationships that helped him to venture out of West Virginia to visit prominent ministries. Jakes met Don Mears, a white Pentecostal pastor of a large congregation in Washington, D.C., called Evangel Temple back in those days, now residing in Maryland as Evangel Cathedral Church. Mears had connections to powerful church leaders and was one of the first well-known pastors to invite Jakes to preach. A current member of Evangel Cathedral reminisced about a more humble image of Jakes preaching in tight suits and high-water pants. Mears endorsed Jakes before he was well known and was influential in connecting him to other prominent preachers on the East Coast.

Jakes traversed beyond West Virginia to preach at small conferences and meetings and began to visit important events that provided strategic networking. The Hampton Ministers and Music Conference was (and still remains) a major event that showcased black Baptist preaching sensations like Gardner C. Taylor and Samuel Proctor. Pastors traveled from all over the nation to hear popular pastors and gospel singers at one of the earliest All-Star arenas for black preaching. The fact that Jakes began visiting the

Hampton Conference in the early 1990s as a curious spectator demonstrates his growing exposure to larger networks outside of West Virginia's borders. Meeting flashy pastors at these prestigious gatherings no doubt provided Jakes some useful cue cards for his incipient reinvention as a cosmopolitan preacher. It must have been a poignant experience for Jakes to keynote the Hampton Conference in 2002 after attending as an unknown spectator more than a decade earlier.

Jakes met the popular pastor Ernestine Reems in the late 1980s through her connection with other pastors on the East Coast. Reems invited Jakes to preach at her church in California, an auspicious opportunity for a relatively unknown West Virginia preacher. Reems is proud to be among the first prominent ministers to invite Jakes to preach and discussed his early visits:

> He was a dynamic speaker then, nobody just had tapped into it and gave him the opportunity, but the man is a gifted and anointed preacher of excellence and our people loved him—they didn't come to church—but they loved him. The second time he came he said afterwards, "I wonder why they didn't come out Ernestine." Well, I didn't have the proper money to advertise him; he wasn't on television yet. I always knew if someone gave him an opportunity he would do what he is doing. (Interview)

Reems was an important friend to Jakes and encouraged him during a period of frustration with ministry. Jakes persevered through the early struggles, and by the early 1990s he was still going strong, still tenaciously pursuing ministry opportunities and still mesmerizing small audiences in West Virginia churches with his uncanny ability to diagnose the human condition.

Reflecting on Jakes' childhood we can see that growing up in the hills of West Virginia shielded him from the harsh urban realities that can stifle a young child's capacity for self-transcendence. Jakes did not have to wrestle with gangs or worry about drive-by shootings, and he was not inundated with the kind of hopelessness that many of his young African American contemporaries faced in the concrete jungles of inner cities. Jakes grew up in a safe community and supportive environment where self-actualization was encouraged and rewarded.

Jakes' current entrepreneurial drive reaches back to his youth as an ambitious peddler of vegetables and Avon products. Jakes learned at an early age that productive behavior and self-sacrifice could reap intriguing benefits. He also acquired entrepreneurial courage by selling his wares and offering his services. No doubt that each episode of selling fish from his father's truck, vegetables from his mother's garden, and Amway products to his neighbors strengthened Jakes' frontier spirit and faith in an American dream that promises limitless possibilities for hard work and tenacity.

Before preaching his first sermon, Jakes' early years helped fashion him with many of the postmodern features that now distinguish his ministry. Developing close friendships with white peers like Paul Lewis provided Jakes with an early yearning for racial diversity. Jakes' parents gave him freedom to explore his own spirituality, and the diversity of Jakes' religious experience prevented him from being indoctrinated into one particular Christian paradigm. His father's illness and death influenced Jakes' soft spot for suffering people, and his early psychology classes laid the groundwork for a therapeutic ministry. His struggles with his frailties imbued in him a passion to urge Christians to be transparent before God and one another. So Jakes' early experiences nurtured the psychological training, respect for the human condition, and iconoclastic vision that would later generate many followers. Today Jakes transcends racial and denominational lines with a postmodern approach that addresses the existential concerns of many people.

Relocating a struggling storefront in Montgomery to an old dilapidated building in Smithers was a courageous move that could have spelled disaster for his early career. Jakes was not passively waiting for his break to fall out of the sky, but repositioned his small church and pursued opportunities to network while enduring tragedies and abject poverty along the way. Jakes' ministry did not commence in the kind of denominational setting or location known for producing celebrity preachers, but his lack of religious structure provided him room to carve out his own niche. Jakes progressed beneath the radar of the religious establishment and had to take a different route through the burgeoning age of mass media and television exposure.

Jakes was a work in progress and benefited from the guidance and support of his aforementioned friends in ministry like Don Mears, Ernestine Reems, and Sherman Watkins. These leaders were important to Jakes' self-reinvention by exposing him to prominent churches, spiritual gatekeepers, and successful ministries. These ministries also provided Jakes with strategic opportunities to exercise his gifts in front of large audiences and confirmed his effective preaching and uncanny ability to impact lives. Visiting the Hampton Conference also helped Jakes' reinvention by introducing him to a world of spiritual celebrities and primetime preaching. Jakes' exposure to larger-than-life pastors at Hampton planted seeds toward his transformation from country preacher draped in tight shirts and colorful suits to the dapper cosmopolitan pastor who now sports Gucci and Armani suits.

Jakes' capitalist courage and frontier spirit led him to take great risks toward greatness. Like the legendary movie character Rocky Balboa, Jakes defied all odds to reach unprecedented success. Rocky was a poor and shadowy hooligan from the streets punching slabs of meat in training sessions to prepare himself for that moment when he would shine against the champion. Similarly, Jakes was a nameless preacher perfecting his craft in coal-mining towns in West Virginia until he attained his big break to transcend anonymity forever. Rocky and Jakes experienced hard times but learned indispensable lessons in those years of struggle that prepared them for the kind of breaks that come only once in a lifetime.

[2]

Once in a Lifetime

Jakes Receives His Big Break

> You better lose yourself in the music, the moment you own it, you better never let it go. You only get one shot, do not miss your chance to blow. This opportunity comes once in a lifetime.   —Eminem

Traditional black churches sing an old gospel hymn with the striking line, "I'm coming up on the rough side of the mountain." This confession is a suitable theme for the humble beginnings of Jakes' preaching career before he received his big break in the early 1990s. Jakes pursued his calling without a clear road to success and thus had to evolve on the spot, receiving help and guidance from friends along the way. By emerging from West Virginia with no preaching pedigree or support from a large denomination, Jakes broke all the rules in becoming one of the most popular preachers today.

Notwithstanding his hard work and ingenuity, without the intervention of a songbird named Sarah Jordan Powell, a business mogul named Paul Crouch, and a celebrity preacher named Carlton Pearson, Jakes might still be preaching in West Virginia's coal-mining towns. Though his persistence was vital during the years of struggle that preceded his big break, Jakes benefited from social capital derived from the endorsements of spiritual power brokers in the Charismatic or neo-Pentecostal world. Reminiscent of John the Baptist preparing the way for Jesus Christ, Crouch and Pearson provided the platform and visibility to introduce the country preacher to the world. Jakes' rapid rise is unimaginable without television exposure and the neo-Pentecostal movement that began to transcend denominational lines.

Neo-Pentecostal Power Brokers

While little Tommy Jakes was enjoying West Virginia's deep blue lakes and unsurpassed beauty of nature, major changes were taking place in the religious landscape that prepared the ground for his emergence almost three decades later. The budding Pentecostal movement of the early 1900s began to produce large, independent traveling ministries in the 1950s that set the stage for what scholars coined the Charismatic movement. More recently it has become identified as neo-Pentecostalism and in the last twenty-five years has become a force in American Protestantism.

Neo-Pentecostalism refers to the contemporary form of the Pentecostal movement that emerged in the latter part of the twentieth century. It puts less emphasis on the baptism of the Holy Spirit and speaking in tongues, and more on the power of the Holy Spirit for healing, prophetic utterances, vibrant worship and music, and prosperity for believers. Generally, Pentecostals adhere to austere prohibitions against dancing, playing cards, going to movies, listening to secular music, dating, and various activities they perceive as indulging in carnality or worldly pleasures. Conversely, neo-Pentecostals are more flexible and emphasize a Christian's freedom to be led by the Spirit in all aspects of life. Hence, neo-Pentecostalism offers a less costly faith than Pentecostalism by removing puritanical asceticism without sacrificing an emphasis on God's power and an appreciation for ecstatic experiences.

While Pentecostalism is organized denominationally, neo-Pentecostalism is loosely organized through networks of like-minded churches called fellowships. More generally, it reflects a worship style and ideology that pervade both mainline and nondenominational congregations nationwide. Though the majority of neo-Pentecostal churches are independent, many of the largest black Baptist and black Methodist churches embrace a neo-Pentecostal style of worship and worldview. The rise of neo-Pentecostalism has led to the blurring of denominational lines by providing many mainliners with common beliefs and practices regarding the power of the Holy Spirit, worship, and music, hence making many Baptists indistinguishable from Methodists and some other denominations. If one theme can surmise neo-Pentecostalism, it is the emphasis on the role of the Holy Spirit to empower Christians to live with health, vitality, prosperity, and productivity. No other religious figure played a more significant role in the growth of neo-Pentecostalism than Oral Roberts.

In the 1950s, Oral Roberts helped neo-Pentecostalism achieve mainstream status by bringing his popular tent revivals into the homes of thousands of Americans through his weekly television broadcasts. Roberts became a national celebrity as an innovator who insisted on racially integrating his tent meetings during a time of intense racial segregation in the South, as his son Richard has discussed:

> In my father's early tent crusades in the late 1940s and early 50s, he was the first man to break the color line with the races in his tent. Wherever he would go he allowed people of any color to sit anywhere they desired in his tent. Now, there were groups of people, especially in the South, who opposed this and did everything in their power to stop him, but he prevailed and blacks came into his crusades by the thousands and sat anywhere they wanted to sit, and he was the first to do that. (Interview)

In 1965, Oral Roberts, having ceased his tent ministry, founded Oral Roberts University (ORU) of which his son Richard is the current president. Many important neo-Pentecostal superstars attended ORU. A former student named Carlton Pearson would later become one of the most recognizable African American religious leaders of the century.

The 1960s and early 1970s brought forth a development that helped neo-Pentecostalism hit mainstream America, namely the proliferation of religious broadcasting networks. Evangelical preachers rushed to the airwaves after a Federal Communications Commission ruling smoothed the progress of their entry (Finke and Stark 1992). While Oral Roberts was airing prime-time specials on national television, neo-Pentecostal entrepreneurs like Pat Robertson and Paul Crouch were building the largest Christian broadcasting networks in the world. Robertson's Christian Broadcasting Network (CBN) and Crouch's Trinity Broadcasting Network (TBN) were later joined by Jim and Tammy Bakker's Praise the Lord (PTL) network, along with a growing number of preachers joining Oral Roberts on national television. Though mainline preachers like Robert Schuller, Jerry Falwell, and Billy Graham utilized television since the 1970s, the distinction of the televangelist quickly became associated with larger than life neo-Pentecostal-type figures like Kathryn Kuhlman, Oral Roberts, Kenneth Copeland, James Robinson, and the most ubiquitous figure, Jimmy Swaggart, whose ministry in the 1980s secured a weekly audience exceeding ten million viewers. These televangelists introduced neo-Pentecostal ideas to millions of viewers.

Print media also contributed to the growth of neo-Pentecostalism. A businessman named Stephen Strang established a multimedia company that played a vital role in the spread of neo-Pentecostalism by publishing seven Christian magazines and reaching millions more through daily updates over the Internet. *Charisma* is the flagship magazine produced by Strang Communications, and by the early 1990s it became one of the most important avenues used by neo-Pentecostals to market conferences and promote their books, videos, and CDs. Strang's magazines produce editorials and articles on important trends and current events in ministries for millions of subscribers and are important machines in the faith industry that promote neo-Pentecostal preachers toward celebrity. Strang Communications also formed Charisma House Books, a publishing company used by leading neo-Pentecostal preachers to disseminate books on worship, faith, and spiritual gifts. Along with Paul Crouch and Pat Robertson, Stephen Strang became and remains one of the most influential neo-Pentecostal power brokers.

The 1990s marked the high point of the spread of neo-Pentecostalism all over the country. While many mainline denominations continued to decline in membership, John Wimber's Vineyard Movement and other new networks and fellowships spread rapidly across the country. Spiritual revivals in Canada as well as powerful outbreaks in Florida and Tulsa drew thousands of participants nationwide, resembling the Azusa Street Revival of 1906 that was responsible for introducing Pentecostalism to America. Faith healers like Benny Hinn, Tim Story, Rodney Howard Brown, and others traveled to hold crusades in major cities, distributing a new interpretation of the function of the Holy Spirit in the lives of believers. Benny Hinn's book, *Good Morning, Holy Spirit*, became a best-seller in 1991 and ignited a new focus on how the Holy Spirit operates. TBN and *Charisma* magazine informed Christians of new religious celebrities and widespread spiritual breakthroughs. By the end of the twentieth century, neo-Pentecostalism had become a major force all over the world.

Television, more than any other medium, provided mass exposure and the ability to launch the ministerial careers of many preachers and thus was essential to the emergence of neo-Pentecostalism as part of the religious mainstream. This is not to diminish the important roles that mainline innovators like John Richard Bryant, Dennis Bennett, Larry Christenson, and J. Rodman Williams played in introducing neo-Pentecostalism to their denominations. But Christian television exposed the country to neo-Pentecostal ideas and practices and influenced middle-class converts and mainliners to join their churches and organizations. Paul Crouch's TBN became the largest Christian

television network and today produces the most Christian programs. Years later, the Daystar Television Network was launched
and quickly became the second largest Christian television network from which preachers would broadcast their services in 150
countries and on more than fifty stations in the United States.

Jim Bakker, Paul Crouch, Oral Roberts, Pat Robertson, and
Jimmy Swaggart became powerful leaders with their large networks, elaborate mailing lists, and huge followings as television
provided unprecedented exposure for evangelists and preachers.
Although African American entertainers were often guests on
Christian television programs throughout the 1970s and 1980s,
black televangelism was a phenomenon slow to emerge. While
Rev. Ike and Fred Price began to preach controversial sermons
about financial prosperity on television stations in several major
cities, there were no African American preachers on national television with name recognition comparable to Roberts, Swaggart,
and Graham. Before African Americans were able to build television ministries in the mid- to late 1990s on TBN and Black Entertainment Television (BET), noted preachers like Richard
Hinton, Joseph Jackson, Gardner Taylor, John Richard Bryant,
and Arthur Brazier gained popularity primarily through denominational networks or radio broadcasting. Television provided a
new avenue to becoming famous by instantly reaching thousands
or millions of people. So instead of slowly progressing to the upper echelon of denominational leadership as a Baptist state president or Methodist bishop, one could quickly emerge as a star in
the black church simply by consistently appearing on national television.

Carlton Pearson and the AZUSA Conference

The rise of black neo-Pentecostal superstardom is somewhat linked
with white neo-Pentecostals' dominance in televangelism. One
obvious reason is that none of the major Christian broadcasting

Carlton Pearson at the AZUSA Conference. *(Photo courtesy of Carlton Pearson)*

networks were run or owned by African Americans. But a more salient reason stems from the fact that white televangelists drew large contingencies of black viewers and supporters. Pat Robertson, Oral Roberts, and Jim Bakker were very much aware that African Americans made up a strong part of their audiences and donor bases. So when they wanted to invite guest singers and preachers on their programs in the 1970s and 1980s who appealed to their black audiences, they sought African Americans who held similar beliefs and practices. Hence, in the 1980s the black Pentecostal preacher Ben Kenchlow became a familiar face on Pat Robertson's *The 700 Club*, and black Pentecostal recording artists like Andrae Crouch, Brenda Davis, the Winans Family, and the Clark Sisters soared in popularity after they performed on Jim and Tammy Bakker's PTL broadcast.

One of the first and most significant African Americans to consistently appear on religious broadcasts was the young and talented singer Carlton Pearson, who accompanied Oral Roberts in the 1970s. Pearson grew in visibility and influence and eventually became a celebrity and important precursor to T.D. Jakes. Carlton Pearson's rise to the top should have come as no surprise to those who were privy to his privileged life as a talented young preacher with a rich ministry heritage. J.A. Blake, a prominent COGIC bishop and member of the General Board, took an early interest in Pearson's career and paved the road for a bright future. J.A. Blake was also the father of Charles Blake, a popular California pastor whose guests and members include celebrities like Magic Johnson, Stevie Wonder, and Denzel Washington. J.A. Blake was Pearson's first mentor, but after graduating from high school, Pearson's decision to attend ORU brought him under the tutelage of one of the most powerful preachers in American Protestantism.

Pearson was a student at ORU in the early 1970s during a time when Oral Roberts was airing specials on prime-time television before millions of Americans and making appearances on popular programs like *The Merv Griffin Show*. Pearson's singing ability earned him a spot among the elite World Action Singers, a team of twelve ORU students who accompanied Roberts on television. Kathie Lee Gifford, the talented singer and former television co-host of *Regis and Kathie Lee*, began her career as a World Action Singer accompanying Oral Roberts all over the world. Singing on television beside Kathie Lee provided Pearson with national exposure:

> At the time I sang in 1972, Oral Roberts was receiving something like 32,000 pieces of mail a day. Oral was the number one Pentecostal and our program would have millions watch our quarterly contact specials with Della Reese or Pearl Bailey and so I was there watching them, appearing with all of them in places like Alaska and London. (Interview)

Oral Roberts took a special liking to Pearson and helped him navigate through the world of neo-Pentecostal power brokers during his ORU experience and early in his preaching career:

> I gained and garnered respect through my association with Oral Roberts and the wider non-black Pentecostal world. Pat Robertson, Jim Bakker, Paul and Jan Crouch, Kathryn Kuhlman, James Robinson, Morris Cerullo, Jack Hayford—all of these people saw me at partner seminars and other ORU-related conferences. Oral put me on the Board of Regents in 1984 and kept me around him. I was on Oral's television specials and I was on his weekly program and I was doing his seminars and was one of the first blacks on nationwide television on a consistent basis. (Ibid.)

Not long after finishing at ORU in 1976, Pearson founded his own church in Tulsa, Oklahoma, called Higher Dimensions. The church grew quickly, while Pearson maintained visibility as a guest on Pat Robertson's show, *The 700 Club*, as an occasional stand-in host for Jim and Tammy Bakker's show *PTL Club*, and later as a frequent host of *Praise the Lord with Paul and Jan Crouch* on TBN. Pearson was the first African American to regularly host a Christian program on national television.

Pearson maximized his influence by functioning as a bridge to introduce prominent black Pentecostal preachers like J.O. Patterson and O.T. Jones to powerful white magnates like Oral Roberts and Paul Crouch. More importantly, after holding successful conferences in the late 1980s, Pearson began the process of forming an interracial yet predominantly black network of neo-Pentecostal churches as his crowning achievement. He named this network the AZUSA Fellowship to commemorate the Azusa Revival of 1906 that introduced Pentecostalism to the country.

Pearson's AZUSA Fellowship was an attempt to revisit the fervor and power of the early Pentecostal revival through a network of like-minded Christians from all over the country. What was more significant than the actual fellowship itself was the annual meeting in April from which the fellowship emerged—the AZUSA Conference—which drew thousands of Christians nationwide from various denominations to hear prominent preachers, talented musicians, and contemporary gospel singers. No other conference was more successful at drawing a diversity of Christian celebrities in the early-1990s than AZUSA, as Pearson noted:

> You could go to Memphis and find COGIC prominent preachers and some of the top musicians but AZUSA attracted black, non-black, contemporary, traditional, the full gamut. You'd have a James Robinson on the same platform with a Shirley Caesar or a Richard Hinton. (Ibid.)

Pearson's high visibility and contacts with television broadcasters facilitated the quick growth of the fellowship after its inception in 1988. It became a network of hundreds of pastors and churches from various denominations. Through Pearson's relationship with Paul Crouch, who strongly wished to appease his black audience, many nightly meetings of conferences were aired live on TBN. Pearson also had close ties with Stephen Strang, whose *Charisma* magazine began to cover AZUSA conferences and offer Pearson ample opportunities for columns and editorials. Pearson was one of the first African Americans to pay $8,000 for a full-page ad in *Charisma* to promote the conference. Consequently, connecting with Pearson and keynoting his conference provided the possibility of national exposure for talented African American preachers like Ernestine Reems, Richard Hinton, O.T. Jones, and a host of others designated by Pearson to preach. Because of the rapid rise of the popularity of AZUSA meetings, Pearson became one of the most influential African Americans during the early to mid-1990s.

It was an honor for preachers and singers to perform at AZUSA's nightly services. A former coordinator for the conference disclosed that a typical honorarium for musicians or singers was $2,500 and generally around $5,000 for preachers. These are modest figures by today's standards after the influx of mega churches and conferences, but these were considerable amounts in the early 1990s for an hour or less of work. What was far more relevant than the honorarium was the television exposure one might receive while appearing at AZUSA. First, keynoting one of the nightly meetings would generate future preaching engagements in large churches which could garner an extra $200,000 in yearly income, as one staff member estimated. It also gave preachers the chance to expose their books and tape series to a wider audience and sell their products. Many ambitious pastors saw how a black preacher from the Bahamas named Myles Monroe who preached at AZUSA in 1991 benefited from the exposure, and some record company executives and preachers attempted to coerce Pearson to let them perform and preach:

Somebody offered me $100,000 if I would let him preach at AZUSA and he followed that by saying, "Do for me what you did for Myles!" And I said, "I did nothing for Myles; we just happened to be live on television, TBN, when he preached. Myles didn't even realize he was going to be on live television preaching about purpose." It got to the place where record companies were actually calling us asking if they could put people on the stage at AZUSA. It became a business thing of course and it still is in most of these conferences. (Ibid.)

To get a glimpse of what a nightly service at AZUSA was like, one should think of Muhammad Ali's classic boxing matches with Joe Frazier or George Foreman. The arenas of those epic battles were flooded with A-list movie stars, athletes, politicians, and business tycoons, and part of the pleasure was basking in the aura of the moment. AZUSA meetings had a similar mystique and quickly became the prime-time event for black neo-Pentecostals. Part of the thrill of attending the nightly meetings was to gaze at the VIP section and get a glimpse at what the prominent preachers and famous gospel singers were wearing. Expensive suits and dazzling dresses were on display as an air of elegance imbued the arena. Those who had the good fortune of attending this grandiose affair could not avoid the feeling that they were part of something exceptional. The glamour and panache at AZUSA meetings did much to give black Pentecostalism a facelift as a movement no longer relegated only to the disenfranchised but appealing to more privileged African Americans.

Jakes and Sarah Jordan Powell

In 1991, while Pearson's prominence reached astonishing heights with his AZUSA Conference, Jakes had the distinguished honor of meeting Sarah Jordan Powell, the noted gospel singer known as the songbird of the Church of God in Christ, at a small conference. In an interview, Powell discussed meeting Jakes:

We were seated together and when I came in he had already come in and we were seated at a table because it was like a dinner conference. And when I sat down he said, "Oh I'm so happy that I finally get to meet you." He said, "I finally get to meet Sarah Jordan Powell." Well I'm always interested in who the other person is so I said, "Tell me about you." And he said, "Oh I'm just a country preacher." (Interview)

Perhaps Jakes' "I'm just a country preacher" response to Powell was a calibrated shtick to camouflage his ambition, not unlike the television detective Colombo's stratagem of using a clumsy style to lull murder suspects toward underestimating his investigative prowess. Jakes' "just a country preacher" routine helped him feign as an innocent and obtuse West Virginian who posed no threat to prominent ministers and singers with large egos and little tolerance for brash competitors. But Jakes knew he was more than just a country preacher; he was a cleric with the talent and passion to become a celebrity and entrepreneur.

Notwithstanding all of his capabilities and aspirations, Jakes' depiction of himself as just a country preacher was not altogether disingenuous when compared to Sarah Jordan Powell. Jakes was in the presence of a well-traveled gospel singer with eight albums to her credit as well as the national Fine Arts Director for the second largest Pentecostal denomination in the world. The songbird had personal relationships with powerful neo-Pentecostals like Carlton Pearson and Oral Roberts and the adoration of many prominent Christians nationwide. Jakes, in contrast, was still an obscure figure, though word about his preaching abilities began to travel throughout West Virginia. Fortunately, Powell was impressed with Jakes, and when he invited her to his church in West Virginia, she graciously accepted.

Powell described Jakes' church as a small building with about fifty or sixty members, a number far below the size of the average audiences graced by her singing ministry. But the trip to West

Virginia provided an opportunity for her to marvel at Jakes' preaching. Powell learned that Jakes was gifted, but she could not have foreseen the vital role she would play in helping Jakes become a celebrity.

Like most black preachers nationwide, Jakes knew about the AZUSA Conference in April and was impressed by the fact that his new ally was a close friend of Carlton Pearson. The conference must have roused his interest because he called Powell a year after she visited his church to discuss coming to AZUSA 92, as she described:

> [Jakes] called and said, "I've always wanted to come to AZUSA and so I'm thinking about coming this year." I said, "Oh, we'd be delighted to have you." He said, "I'll call you when I get there," so he did, he called me from the hotel. (Ibid.)

The fact that he contacted Powell and decided to attend the conference was seemingly a calculated move on Jakes' part. AZUSA conferences were held in Tulsa, Oklahoma, and hence purchasing a plane ticket and hotel reservation for almost a week during a struggling time in his career was a dicey investment. But Jakes anticipated the networking possibilities that could happen at AZUSA 92 with Powell at his side, so he made the trip. As all of his years of relocating churches indicated, Jakes was not passively waiting for his big break to fall out of the sky but was relentlessly pursuing opportunities to network and expose his name, and perceived AZUSA 92 as another opportunity toward that end.

The moment Jakes arrived at Tulsa's small airport he must have sensed something brewing in the air. AZUSA was a big event in Tulsa each year, and limos flooded the small airport to pick up prominent preachers attending from all over the nation. Very few events brought as many African American tourists to Tulsa as Pearson's yearly meetings. AZUSA 91 had been a big success, and thousands of people cashed in their vacation days and hit Tulsa for AZUSA 92 to attend seminars during the day and to experience prime-time preaching from Fred Price, Richard Hinton, and other prominent speakers each night of the week.

The conference was held in the Mabee Center on the campus of ORU. At other times it had been the preferred venue for Frank Sinatra, the Judds, and other major concerts in the city because of its large seating capacity. On account of Oral Roberts' vast influence, ORU became a sort of Mecca where neo-Pentecostals could pay homage. The building reverberated with a high-tech commercialism that must have overwhelmed Jakes as he passed by long tables selling tapes, videos, and CDs before stepping into the main arena with its television cameras and many lights. Undoubtedly, like the Hampton Conference, this experience provided Jakes an early blueprint for constructing his conferences a few years later.

Jakes attended the first night alone. There was no preferred seating for unknown country preachers, so he made his way high up into the bleachers and soaked up the ambiance among 11,000 anxious spectators. Rather than begging for his autograph or praising his preaching prowess, people simply stepped over Jakes to get to their seats because he had not yet escaped anonymity. In retrospect, it is poetic to visualize the future luminary as just another spectator lost in the crowd. Jakes reminisced:

> It was my first Azusa conference, and I was so excited to see the diversity of people of all faiths and backgrounds gathered together in one concert of praise and worship. What an exhilarating experience it was for me! I was not a speaker, a singer, or on the program at all. I was just another face in the place. (Jakes 2002:17)

After attending the first night alone, Jakes called Powell from his hotel to ask if he could ride with her and her husband John the second night. She agreed, and Jakes attended the Tuesday night service side-by-side with a neo-Pentecostal star of great repute and unknowingly began the journey toward his big break. Jakes arrived at the Mabee Center with Sarah and John almost an hour early, at 6:00 P.M., which was still tardy considering that the auditorium was already swarming with enthusiastic worshipers. The Chicago preaching veteran Richard Hinton was the speaker for the night, and the excitement was palpable. Jakes and the Powells walked to the VIP section and met the usher whose task was to lead prominent figures to reserved seating. This usher was Vanessa Weatherspoon, who at the time was a seminary student at ORU and has since become a well-known preacher. Weatherspoon was happy to seat her friends Sarah and John but noticed a problem concerning their guest, as Powell recalled:

> When we arrived the place was already jammed. It was like six in the evening and the usher said to my husband and me, "I have seats for you, come quickly." I told her we have a guest with us but she said, "We only have two seats; it's very crowded." (Interview)

Weatherspoon also recalled her first encounter with the country preacher from West Virginia:

> When Jakes first came to AZUSA I was working the floor and Sarah came late. I remember telling Sarah I don't have but two seats. She said, "I've got this guest here from West Virginia," and I was like, "I'm sorry but I can't put y'all up there." (Interview)

Jakes offered to throw in the towel and make a lonely trek back to the same spot he sat the night before, but Sarah insisted they sit together. Her renown paid off because another usher found three seats for them in the front row.

Jakes was no longer up in the rafters like the previous night. Now he was close enough to see the sweat drop from the preacher's face. Jakes was just soaking up the grandeur, as Powell discussed:

> T.D. was like a little boy. He sat there with his chin in his hand saying, "Oh this is wonderful, this service is just awesome." He was

so animated; he was just like a little kid, he kept saying, "I'm en-joying this so much." (Ibid.)

Jakes was having a taste of the stardom and greatness he craved since he was a child. While listening to Hinton's sermon, he must have envisioned himself behind the glass pulpit, just like young pop singers fantasize accepting a Grammy award. AZUSA exem-plified one of the ultimate achievements of one's preaching ca-reer, so Jakes must have wondered if an unknown preacher from West Virginia could ever grace the stage.

Hinton's sermon had a profound effect on Jakes because he "used an analogy that became a precursor for how the Lord was about to use and bless me and my ministry" (Jakes 2000:16). Hinton was preaching about the turning of the stage when God will propel Christians into challenging leadership positions that far exceed their expectations. At the time Jakes was unaware of how prophetic Hinton's analogy was with respect to his own life. An hour after the service and six months after the conference his ministry would change.

The songbird really went to bat for Jakes in more ways than one. Not only did she insist on sitting with him, but she also de-cided to introduce Jakes to Carlton Pearson at the end of the service. A person familiar with AZUSA in the early 1990s under-stands the daunting task of trying to speak with Carlton Pearson after a nightly service. Pearson was the leading light, the visionary who started the fellowship and conference, the one who, with na-tional exposure, could carry an ambitious preacher to stardom. Pearson was the adopted son in ministry of the de facto pope of neo-Pentecostalism, Oral Roberts. Pearson was at the height of his popularity and it was not a mystery what meeting him could do for one's career. Once the service was over, pastors from all over the country, friends, family members, and gospel music stars swarmed the backstage area coveting the opportunity to kiss Pearson's ring, so to speak. But Powell made up her mind to lead Jakes to Pearson.

Jakes groused at the difficult task ahead of them, but Powell knew that with perseverance they would reach their objective. As they drew near the back where all the people were gathering, they reencountered Vanessa Weatherspoon, and Powell told her, "I need you to get me to the back because this is somebody that I have to make sure Pastor Carlton gets to meet." The Powells and their guest then advanced toward the room where Pearson was greeting people. A security guard greeted them and opened the door to show them the hundreds of people waiting to see Pearson. After Powell explained her wish to introduce her guest to Pearson, the security guard relented and let them through. Finally, almost an hour later, they came within reach of Pearson.

Powell's persistence set the stage for one of the most important introductions in the history of the black church. Pearson gave them his undivided attention. According to Powell:

> I said to Pastor Carlton, "This is Bishop Jakes. He's a wonderful man of God. He's an anointed preacher and I just really wanted him to get to meet you." So Bishop Jakes said, "How do you do?" in his inimitable voice, and so Pastor Carlton said, "My, he really has the preacher's voice." (Interview)

Pearson reminisced about the night he met Jakes after he had shaken hands with pastors from all over the country:

> Sarah was one of the last ones in and she was with Jakes. He looked young and shy and sort of bashful, didn't say hardly anything. I remember his voice was real raspy and I brushed my fingers across his throat and said, "You sound like you can preach." (Interview)

Powell recalled how she made a passionate attempt to convince Pearson he needed to invite Jakes to preach:

I said, "You really really would be so blessed by his ministry. He's a powerful man of God, loves Jesus very much and it would be wonderful if he could come back to Tulsa and minister at the church." So [Pearson] said, "Maybe we can look forward to that happening." So Pastor Carlton asked me for a tape and Bishop Jakes gave me that, and I shared it with pastor. (Interview)

Pearson met many eager preachers that night but remembered Jakes and took his tape very seriously because the songbird was his advocate. Pearson had admired Powell since his youth, so her presence with Jakes captured his attention. If Jakes had been accompanied by anyone else, his meeting with Pearson would have been less significant. For example, Don Mears, a prominent preacher in Maryland, later reminded his good friend Pearson that he had already tried to sell him on Jakes a few years before Powell had introduced him at AZUSA. Pearson told Mears he did not remember the conversation because he received hundreds of such submissions about preachers from all over the country. Thus Pearson credits Sarah Jordan Powell's wonderful late-night introduction of Jakes at AZUSA 92 as the catalyst behind the greater things that resulted from their connection.

Jakes was able to meet other leading ministers at the conference, including an up-and-coming preacher from New Jersey named Donald Hilliard. The two became good friends, and Hilliard called on Jakes to preach at his installation service to the bishopric in 1995. But the highlight of Jakes' journey to Tulsa was meeting Carlton Pearson, the man who would soon serve as the bridge to carry him over the chasm between anonymity and eminence. Overall, AZUSA 92 was a special moment in Jakes' life. The sacrifices he made to make the trip to Tulsa would produce dividends a few months later when Pearson set the ball rolling for Jakes' big break.

Behind Closed Doors

While Jakes spent the next few months conducting public therapy sessions for women through Sunday School lessons at his church in Charleston, West Virginia, Sarah Jordan Powell was making sure that Pearson would open doors for Jakes' ministry. A few weeks after AZUSA 92, Powell visited Pearson's home and inquired about Jakes' tape, which she had given him at the conference. Pearson had listened to the tape and was very impressed and told Powell he would invite Jakes to preach at his church, Higher Dimensions (known to most as Higher D). This pleased Powell, who knew that preaching at Higher D could only increase the prospects for Jakes' promising career.

Not many country preachers are afforded personal introductions to one of the most powerful ministers, and even fewer are afforded invitations to preach at his church. Speaking at Higher D was the trial run to see if Jakes was ready to step up to the plate. Pearson aired segments of his church services on a thirty-minute weekly television program on TBN, so this opportunity also had the potential for national exposure for Jakes if he chose to air Jakes' segment. Jakes had been aggressively pursuing his break for years, and this was the kind of opportunity he craved.

Pearson decided that Jakes would not preach for a Sunday worship service, but instead appointed him to keynote a regional meeting of ministerial leaders of the AZUSA Fellowship in October of 1992 called the Pastors Ministers and Workers Conference. Pearson held these small quarterly meetings at his church for the pastors and ministers associated with his fellowship. Jakes, Mark Hanby, and Brian Keith Williams were the three guest speakers selected by Pearson for the small conference affectionately called "mini-AZUSA" by those affiliated with the fellowship. Mark Hanby, a white Pentecostal, was gaining momentum in the South for his spirited messages and clever preaching. Brian Keith

Williams resembled Malcolm X in his tall commanding stature and rapid-fire delivery, and his signature was a witty use of alliteration. Hanby and Williams eventually became distinguished preachers but, like Jakes, were relatively unknown at this point in their careers. Pearson used the small leadership conference as an early springboard for young promising preachers to eventually keynote the main event in April.

Williams preached Wednesday night, Hanby on Thursday, and Jakes had the task of closing out the conference on Friday night. On Jakes' night there were only about five hundred people in attendance at Higher D, and the normally filled balcony was empty. William Abney sang a melodious rendition, and Pearson followed with a colorful introduction, informing the audience that Sarah Jordan Powell was the mastermind behind Jakes' appearance at Higher D. Jakes was wearing a copper-colored double-breasted suit that was apparently too tight and had an iron-shined look that dark suits tend to get from excessive ironing. A few years later Jakes wrote about wearing such suits during these humble days:

> I even preached in suits that shined. They shined not because they were in style, but because they were worn, pressed with an iron, and eventually washed in the washing machine because cleaners were out of the question. (Jakes 1994b:108)

Jakes must have been very nervous because his shirt was visibly soaked with perspiration, but he broke the tension with a slick joke about his wife being his girlfriend and the audience laughed. Jakes settled down and preached a resounding message called "Behind Closed Doors," and the people were blessed, which was the typical outcome of his ministry. Carlton Pearson was especially pleased with the sermon because it set off a spiritual breakthrough in his sister's life and provided healing in their relationship. But the more important fact for Jakes was that "Behind Closed Doors" provided his first national exposure. Pearson decided to play segments of Hanby, Williams, and Jakes' sermons on his television program, and his production staff took great care to edit them down to seven-minute clips portraying each preacher at his best. Jakes admitted he was unaware that Pearson was going to play his message on his television show, and he was equally oblivious to the relevance of that decision. Jakes reminisced years later at AZUSA 2000:

> I didn't know anything about television. I came up in the hills of West Virginia. I knew more about storefronts than television. I didn't know what they were going to do with the message.

Though Pearson's show was quite popular, seven minutes on national television was generally not nearly enough exposure to change one's career, but Jakes believes that God intervened to make them the seven most momentous minutes of his life. Paul Crouch, the founder and president of TBN, arrived at his home after a tiring day of intense contemplation, plunged down on the sofa, and turned on the television at the very same time that his station aired Pearson's broadcast of Jakes' seven-minute clip. Crouch was wrestling with an important decision about his autobiography and found the solution in Jakes' clipped sermon, as Jakes recalled:

> And it just so happened that Paul was writing a book, *I Had No Father But God*, and he was trying to wrestle with whether to tell the whole story or not and it just so happened that at the right seven minutes, they picked the right seven parts of my message at the right time to touch his heart, to make him weep. (Ibid.)

Jakes had no misconceptions about the fortuitous timing that allowed him to capture Crouch's attention and what that meant to his career. He continued:

If the editor in the editing suite would have used another clip out of the message, if Paul would have stopped for a ham sandwich, if you [Jakes points to Carlton Pearson] would have decided, "I'm not going to put it on the air," if I would have preached another sermon that night, then none of this would have happened. (Ibid.)

Crouch was so overwhelmed by Jakes' seven-minute clip that he immediately called Pearson to inquire about the unknown guest preacher, as Pearson recounted:

So Paul called me and said, "Who was the man you had on and I need to hear that entire message?" And I said, "Would you like to have the master?" "Would you air it if I sent it to you," and he said, "Yes." (Interview)

Pearson immediately sent Crouch the master tape. Now the president of the largest Christian television network in the world had Jakes' magnum opus, "Behind Closed Doors." This meant that one of the most powerful men in Christendom had the sermon of the unknown country preacher who came from humble beginnings, the man who dug ditches until his hands bled to support his family a few years earlier; the storefront preacher who shuffled his church three times on his journey to greatness. Crouch was true to his promise and played Jakes' hour-long sermon on his broadcasting network for a large Christian audience to see in its entirety. Crouch did not just play the entire sermon once, but every Friday night for eight weeks. A buzz about Jakes began to spread across the country. This was part 1 of Jakes' ascent.

AZUSA 93

Crouch's airtime gave Jakes his first sample of national exposure. Carlton Pearson was well aware of the thrill that TBN created for Jakes and decided to help him maintain his momentum by inviting him back to Higher D in February 1993 to preach the Sunday morning and night services. Jakes preached his now classic sermon, "The Puppet Master," delineating how God works behind the scenes for believers in a manner resembling a puppet master pulling strings. A few weeks later, while on a speaking tour in England, Pearson decided to call Jakes and invite him to speak at the main event, the AZUSA Conference in April.

Jakes was both very excited and nervous about his invitation to speak at AZUSA 93. He knew he would be bumping elbows with high-rollers sporting fancy suits and thousand-dollar shoes. He had already proven that he was a gifted preacher, but was he ready for the big time? Wasn't he just a visitor lost in the crowd at AZUSA 92 a year earlier? Jakes knew that keynoting this prominent conference could generate many preaching engagements at large churches nationwide. After his experience with Paul Crouch playing his message on TBN, Jakes was no longer naive about what television exposure could do for his career. He knew that many AZUSA services were aired live on TBN, and since he had previously impressed Crouch, another classic sermon could produce tremendous momentum for his budding fame. But opportunity and risk go hand-in-hand, and Jakes also knew that striking out could impede his progress. Was he just a one-hit wonder? Jakes considered many things as he prepared for his big moment.

Jakes also had the important task of deciding what to preach. What do you preach when you receive the opportunity of a lifetime? What do you preach to make a profound impact at AZUSA 93? Well, Jakes cleverly decided to preach "Woman Thou Art

Loosed," a sermon that was sparked by his successful Sunday School lessons back in West Virginia. The public forums at his church in which women discussed personal problems and struggles helped Jakes develop a unique sensitivity to them. Since the pews of black churches nationwide are filled predominantly by black women, it was a savvy choice for Jakes to channel his gifts toward their common struggles.

The time had come in April 1993 for Jakes to have his second big moment with destiny. One could feel the tension in the air. Some people had already seen Jakes on TBN and were waiting to hear from this mysterious preacher who virtually came out of nowhere to pique their curiosity. The auditorium was jam-packed on this closing night of the conference. Early in the evening AZUSA workers called Pearson at home to inform him they were out of room and had to turn people away. Pearson told them to pull the curtains down and fill every available seat. As a result, over 12,000 people came in that night to hear Jakes. All eyes were on the country preacher from West Virginia as he walked across the stage beneath the blinding lights. Jakes later reminisced about how AZUSA 93 introduced him to the next twenty years of living—the part of him that was waiting in the wings (Jakes 2002).

Those whose eyes had never gazed upon Jakes must have been puzzled by the six-foot-three, 300-plus-pound preacher who graced the stage. This was before Jakes lost a hundred pounds and before he could afford Italian suits, fancy jewelry, and a $2 million home. This was before he was the celebrity preacher, movie producer, playwright, and best-selling author. This was before he appeared on the cover of *Time* magazine, and before over 130,000 people came to his family vacation event in Atlanta. This was the humble preacher trying to carve out a space for himself with a spiritual yet profoundly human message of empowerment.

Jakes set the pace with a passionate prayer asking God's power and glory to touch the service:

Spirit of the living God, breathe in this place. Release an anointing because somebody in this room is in trouble. Somebody's wife is in trouble, some mother of the church, some first lady is in trouble; encumbered with duties and responsibilities. Functioning like a robot but bleeding like a wounded dog . . . I pray that in the name of Jesus the Holy Ghost would release a glory in this place— that an earthquake would start in this room and reverberate across the country into every city, state, and town.

He then began his historic sermon by discussing how terrible it is to be in trouble when you are in church because "we make people think that when you're in the church you're not supposed to be in trouble." Jakes continued with his trademark blend of theatrical preaching and emotional therapy to exhort his listeners to be free from all that bound them. He urged women not to let others define them but to use their special gifts and talents, celebrate their uniqueness, and be open and honest about their pain in order to seek healing from God.

No doubt many in attendance had never heard of Jakes before AZUSA 93, but after his stunning success he became a name most will never forget. Thousands of women were jumping, screaming, and crying because Jakes had put his finger on their pain. Some were awestruck in catatonic stupors after being mesmerized by his message. Others raced to the tables to purchase tapes and videos of the sermon which ended up selling over $20,000 worth of products, according to Pearson. No other male preacher had diagnosed women's struggles so eloquently and effectively, and no one with such precision had ever articulated women's anguish. Before the night started, Jakes' destiny was on the balance and now the scales tipped in his favor and he was on his way to becoming a star.

Like the Puerto Rican vocalist Ricky Martin's appearance at the 1999 Grammy Awards propelled his career to unforeseeable heights, Jakes' masterpiece at AZUSA 93 would quickly launch him like a missile. Pastors from all over the country were trying to book him to preach at their large churches. Paul Crouch contacted him about broadcasting his sermons on TBN. The Jakes phenomenon began and has yet to cease in momentum. It is hard to fathom that an unknown preacher came to AZUSA 92 as a spectator lost in the crowd, and left the same conference one year later a virtual celebrity.

Jakes' amazing rise is embedded in historical moments and opportunity structures that brought his individual initiative to bear. By the 1980s Oral Roberts, Jimmy Swaggart, and various other neo-Pentecostal preachers developed international ministries by broadcasting their church services on television. The early 1990s marked the time when neo-Pentecostalism began to explode across the nation and transcend denominational lines through television exposure and print media. New technology, commercial networks, and mass media communications converged as part of a neo-Pentecostal revolution out of which Jakes was able to emerge. Jakes' big break and consequent rise in popularity converged with a surfacing faith industry that was turning preachers like Benny Hinn and Carlton Pearson into celebrities.

Carlton Pearson provided African American preachers a platform for national exposure through his AZUSA conferences as well as legitimizing the black genre of preaching and gospel presentation for a wider American audience. AZUSA attracted participants from various denominations and displayed the high-tech commercialism that would characterize Jakes' future ministry and entrepreneurial endeavors. Years later, Jakes wrote his best-seller, *Maximize the Moment*, urging people to realize that opportunities come and go and so they must be ready to capitalize on them. The theme of that book was already in place when Jakes successfully seized the moment at AZUSA in 1993 to ignite his national ministry.

Jakes' dramatic rise represents a new era in which preachers can become celebrities virtually overnight through television exposure rather than denominational positioning. After his big break at AZUSA, Jakes became the symbol of a flourishing new black

church that no longer takes its cues from mainliners and flour-
ishes with mega ministries and financial portfolios that rival entire
denominations. Although the country preacher began his career
in a traditional Pentecostal context, AZUSA helped Jakes take a
big step toward reinventing himself as a cosmopolitan neo-Pentecostal superstar while becoming a prophetic sign and wonder.

[3]

Prophetic Sign and Wonder
Jakes' Ministry Explodes

At that time Jakes was fat, sweating, wearing shiny bright color suits, I mean nothing slick and suave about him. God took a man like this and made him our hero. From his meager background of poverty and his daddy dying when he was young, for God to take a person like that and confound the world is a prophetic sign and wonder.   —Carlton Pearson

It is ironic that two contemporaries like Thomas Jakes and Carlton Pearson ascended to similar heights by way of strikingly contrasting journeys. Pearson was a cosmopolitan Californian; Jakes was a country boy from West Virginia. Young Carlton was self-assured; young Thomas wrestled with low self-esteem. Preaching came easy for Carlton; Thomas struggled early on with a lisp. Carlton was a high school student body president; Thomas was a high school dropout.

In the early 1970s, Carlton Pearson was swimming in Oral Roberts' pool while Thomas Jakes was watching his father slowly die. In the early 1980s, Pearson was traveling in limos and jets, preaching in almost every denominational setting, while Jakes was digging ditches with hemorrhaging hands to feed his family. Pearson was destined for success, while Jakes' future was far less certain. But what Jakes lacked in strategic positioning, he overcompensated in the drive, talent, and postmodern features

T. D. Jakes at the AZUSA Conference in 2000. *(Photo courtesy of Carlton Pearson)*

that would propel his ministry to a unique place in American Protestantism.

During the early 1990s, Carlton Pearson had a virtual monopoly on getting black neo-Pentecostals to spend their money and vacation time attending yearly conferences. But other preachers soon followed his lead and established conferences that competed with AZUSA. For example, a popular New Orleans pastor named Paul Morton decided to organize the Full Gospel Baptist Church Fellowship a year after attending Pearson's AZUSA meeting. Morton knew that the National Baptist Convention was losing ground as the largest African American denomination. Morton was also aware of Pearson's success at drawing many black Baptists to the AZUSA Conference, and so he organized a fellowship and yearly conference for Baptists sympathetic to the neo-Pentecostal worship experience. Morton's first meeting in 1995 drew over 20,000 Baptists.

Publicly and privately, Morton thanked Pearson for teaching black pastors how to present a national conference because AZUSA set the standard for the proliferation of other fellowships and national meetings that followed in the mid 1990s. Darryl Grant, a pastor in Charlotte, North Carolina discussed how AZUSA introduced a high-tech neo-Pentecostalism to aspiring pastors nationwide who soon learned that marketing and business savvy could be fruitful elements in their ministries. Pearson was also the first African American to advertise his conferences on national television and to place expensive ads in *Charisma*, the popular Christian magazine through which Oral Roberts, Benny Hinn, Kenneth Copeland, and other prominent white neo-Pentecostals marketed their events. If one takes a quick glance through a recent issue of *Charisma*, one will see African American preachers advertising an array of conferences in cities nationwide.

T.D. Jakes' ascent is almost unimaginable without his fortuitous encounters with Carlton Pearson and AZUSA. Although none quite equaled his fame, Jakes is not the only preacher to become a superstar after performing at AZUSA. The pastor and

T.D. Jakes, Carlton Pearson, and Paul Morton. *(Photo courtesy of Carlton Pearson)*

Grammy Award–winning gospel singer Donnie McClurkin credited his appearances at AZUSA in the early 1990s for launching his career. Myles Monroe, a virtual unknown before preaching at AZUSA, went on to sell hundreds of thousands of books after keynoting the conference in 1991. Joyce Meyer had been on the radio for many years but did not become nationally known until she preached at AZUSA 93 and now sells millions of books and videos annually. Juanita Bynum, Brian Keith Williams, and Mark Hanby also expanded their ministries and influence after preaching at AZUSA in the 1990s. The defamed televangelist Jim Bakker jumpstarted his comeback at AZUSA 95 only two days after his release from a humbling prison stint. With the exception of Bakker, these preachers were virtually unknown before appearing at AZUSA and later became celebrities through the same faith industry that propelled Jakes into stardom. Pearson discussed his important role in launching the careers of many people:

> Years ago the Lord once told me that I would be a bridge between the nations, cultures, races, and denominations. I wrote it down and began to weep and rejoice and dance. And then God said, "But remember, bridges get walked over and run over and in fact they're not functioning unless they're giving access." So when you talk about Donnie McClurkin, Jakes, Myles, and all these people that have walked across the stage of AZUSA and suddenly have become household names, that's part of the thing God spoke would be one of the traits of my ministry, which is that I would bridge people to their destiny and to each other. (Interview)

The AZUSA Fellowship peaked in the mid-1990s, but today it is in decline. Carlton Pearson lost his prominent role partly due to competition from conferences and fellowships by the very preachers he helped launch, but largely due to his recent embrace of a controversial doctrinal position. Pearson's message of universal reconciliation, a liberal doctrine better known as the "gospel of inclusion" because it asserts all humans are saved by Christ's atoning work on the cross, exceeded the tolerance of those in his evangelical circles. Even Oral Roberts, Charles Blake, and Jakes recently disparaged his teachings. The superstar whom ambitious black preachers once coveted nationwide has within the last few years become a preacher of disrepute. Notwithstanding his fall from grace, Carlton Pearson's place is secure in history as the man who brought Jakes and others to stardom, a role for which Ernestine Reems remains grateful:

> I love Carlton and Carlton should be loved by all of us because he helped all of us. He sure did help me because more doors just swung open; they really just swung open. We should be honest about the thing. Carlton helped T.D. Jakes, he helped Juanita Bynum, he helped Jackie McCullough; he got a lot of them on TBN—they wouldn't have got on there without Carlton. Some of us forget the bridge that carried us over! Don't act like you came all up by yourself somewhere out of the blue skies! (Interview)

Like John the Baptist's death was an important antecedent of Jesus Christ's public ministry, Carlton Pearson's decline made room for Jakes to become the most prolific African American spiritual leader of our time.

The Jakes Phenomenon

Jakes' sermon "Woman Thou Art Loosed" was a resounding hit and, as he noted, it was the launching pad for bigger and brighter days:

> Shortly after I preached the closing night at Azusa, one opportunity after another began to fall into my path. Owners of the Trinity Broadcast Network contacted me about broadcasting my sermons. (Jakes 2002:18)

Though his good fortune with TBN and AZUSA materialized through chance and charity, Jakes took big risks and made calculated decisions to build on his momentum. He was not the first preacher to be given a national platform from AZUSA, but he is the only one who developed the organizational structure and business savvy to become perhaps the most influential spiritual leader of our time.

The annual AZUSA Conference had become such a success that Carlton Pearson decided to experiment with additional conferences on both coasts in 1993. In August, Pearson held a conference in Atlanta called AZUSA East and invited Jakes again as one of the keynotes. In November, Pearson brought Jakes to AZUSA West at the Faith Dome in California, which at the time was the largest church building in America built by an African American pastor. Both conferences were successful, and Jakes dazzled thousands more with his preaching. Jakes was accepting invitations to preach at mega churches nationwide as his momentum continued to increase.

While Jakes quickly became a hit on the national preaching circuit, TBN was broadcasting his sermons. According to Pearson, Paul Crouch was resolute in satisfying TBN's black audience and saw Jakes as a talented vehicle toward that end. Jakes excelled on TBN and wrote a book a few months later in 1993 with the same title as his Sunday School lesson and breakthrough sermon, "Woman Thou Art Loosed." This book addressed taboo subjects in churches concerning women's struggles with molestation, divorce, and depression.

Jakes used much of his own money procured from speaking engagements to publish the book with Destiny Image, a small Christian publishing company. Although the publisher wanted to use a different title, Jakes insisted on using the title of his classic sermon, thus demonstrating his early desire to control his entrepreneurial destiny. His investment quickly paid off because the book sold out less than a month after its first printing. Jakes continued to promote his book on TBN and in speaking engagements nationwide. Book sales rapidly exceeded 200,000, making it one of the best-selling Christian books in the nation, but more importantly signifying that Jakes was on the rise.

One year later, in 1994, Jakes' ministry was expanding rapidly and the need to develop a machine to organize his ministerial endeavors was apparent. While still pastoring his church in West Virginia, Jakes established T.D. Jakes Ministries and moved his television program to Sunday night on TBN, a premier time slot previously occupied by Carlton Pearson. It cost $30,000 a month for that coveted slot, so Pearson had decided to cancel his contract with TBN. The fact that Jakes was able to take over this slot demonstrates his early organizational savvy and financial acuity. Jakes knew that television exposure was the key to fanning the flames of his budding celebrity, so T.D. Jakes Ministries became his money-generating nonprofit machine to fuel his payments. TBN gave Jakes some early slack because Paul Crouch desperately wanted to maintain the black audience that Pearson had acquired while in that time slot.

Jakes called his show *Get Ready with T.D. Jakes*, reliving his famous catch phrase that propelled him to stardom the closing night of AZUSA 93. He added weekly broadcasts on Black Entertainment Television (BET), which also increased his exposure. Jakes avoided being typecast as just a preacher for women by establishing his first yearly conference for men called "Manpower," drawing thousands to Detroit in 1994. Jakes also was a speaker for two stadium events for Promise Keepers, a popular series of meetings and gatherings of mostly white evangelical men, demonstrating that Jakes' popularity was extending beyond black churches. It was clear to all onlookers that the Jakes phenomenon had begun.

Jakes learned a lesson from the $20,000 worth of products that were sold from his appearance at AZUSA 93, which was that his name and message could be used to generate tremendous wealth. He established T.D. Jakes Enterprises as the for-profit apparatus to produce and market his products. Jakes wrote more books and produced videos of his sermons, and Christian bookstores nation-wide could not keep his products on their shelves for too long. By April of 1995 Jakes had written five books and launched a nation-ally syndicated radio version of his television broadcast. After reaching great success with "Woman Thou Art Loosed" as a Sun-day School lesson, breakthrough sermon at AZUSA, and best-selling book, Jakes began holding conferences for women around the country with the same title. These annual conferences would have the predominant role in securing Jakes' unprecedented es-teem with women. He was now popular enough to compete with Pearson's AZUSA 95, drawing seven thousand people to Charleston, West Virginia, for his Back to the Bible conference in the same month. Jakes began to draw noted speakers and per-formers such as Jackie McCullough, Creflo Dollar, and Shirley Caesar to tap into the neo-Pentecostal market share previously monopolized by Pearson.

Delores Carpenter, a pastor and scholar in Washington, D.C., discussed Jakes' early decision to hold his own independent events back in the mid-1990s:

> Bishop Jakes claimed that no church in D.C. was big enough for him. He had been to Greater Mt. Calvary and Jericho and he wanted to do his own thing. You know, like Billy Graham comes in and organizes, you come and send your front people out and or-ganize your own meeting, so it was his first time trying to do it in-dependently. (Interview)

Carpenter discussed how Jakes held a breakfast for pastors from the D.C. area to request their assistance in organizing an event and spreading the word in the capital. Jakes' skill at mobilizing lo-cal pastors for his events in cities nationwide would remain an es-sential trait of his career. Similarly, his ability to market his message and ministry was crucial to his success.

Jakes continued crisscrossing the preaching circuit, appearing on national television four times a week and writing books with several Christian publishers. All of this occurred while he was still pastoring his church, Temple of Faith, whose membership almost tripled to a thousand after his newfound fame. Because of his hectic traveling schedule, Jakes was rarely preaching at his church on consecutive Sundays. Members who were accustomed to a comfortable level of access and personal attention from him before his big break now had to share him with an influx of new members and the demands of his growing ministry.

By 1995, book sales, speaking engagements, conferences, and video sales made Jakes a millionaire. He began to flaunt his riches by enjoying a first-class lifestyle. Jakes had become a virtual celebrity in West Virginia and correspondingly faced media scrutiny. Scathing editorials in local newspapers criticized Jakes for purchasing expensive cars and a mansion with an indoor bowling alley and an indoor swimming pool. The negative media attention angered Jakes and prompted him eventually to relocate his family to Texas to start a new church. It was clear that his ministry had outgrown West Virginia and notwithstanding the negative publicity, Jakes' move to Dallas was strategic for several reasons.

First, the airport of a major city like Dallas was better suited for rigorous traveling to and from his speaking engagements and conferences nationwide. Second, with a new church and better production capabilities, Jakes could record shows for television at his church rather than on the road as necessitated when he was in West Virginia. Third, Jakes could increase his membership in a larger city like Dallas. Fourth, TBN had a location in Dallas, making it easier for Jakes to interact with the network. These justifications for his move to Dallas in the summer of 1996 aside, it was the bad taste in his mouth from negative local publicity that provoked Jakes to leave. As one close friend put it, "Tommy would have never left West Virginia if they would have treated him right."

By the summer of 1996, Jakes had written over twelve successful books, appeared on television four times a week, distributed videos of his sermons nationwide, and drew tens of thousands of Christians to his conferences. Meanwhile, Jakes, his staff, and over fifty families moved to Dallas to start a new church called the Potter's House. Temple of Faith had a jubilant celebration for their beloved former pastor, and even the governor of West Virginia attended the going-away service, asserting that he had become a fan of Jakes. Quickly after his repositioning to Dallas, Jakes' new start-up church purchased a five-thousand-seat building for $3.2 million from W.V. Grant, the defamed televangelist who had just received a sixteen-month prison term for using church funds as a down payment on a million-dollar estate without reporting it as taxable income. Grant's church and television ministry went downhill after ABC's *Prime Time Live* exposed his luxurious lifestyle and alleged chicanery, including fabricating prophetic words about healings and lying about supporting orphanages in Haiti.

The move to Dallas immediately irritated many local pastors who were aware of Jakes' ability to draw members from their congregations. Such dissent was not without merit because almost two thousand people joined the Potter's House on its opening Sunday. By November of the same year, *Charisma* magazine described Jakes as one of the nation's most popular preachers. The Potter's House quickly became one of the fastest-growing churches in the country, and by the end of the year had over eight thousand members. The challenges that came with explosive growth and adjustment to new urban dynamics were daunting for a preacher from the hills of West Virginia, but Jakes was a quick study and never looked back.

In 1997, Jakes celebrated his fortieth birthday by purchasing a new blue convertible BMW. Deciding he was too valuable a marketing commodity to remain plump, he shed almost a hundred pounds to accommodate his new flamboyant attire. A trimmer Jakes capitalized on his transformation by releasing a book called *Lay Aside the Weight*, which offered five principles for shedding pounds. Jakes would later gain some of the weight back but never returned to the portly image of his early preaching days. In the same year the magazine *Christianity Today* acknowledged that Jakes' new church was one of America's fastest growing.

Jakes received great media attention in 1997 when he baptized four football players from the Dallas Cowboys. News cameras filled the Potter's House to record the flashy cornerback Deion Sanders performing a two-step in the water, and running back Emmit Smith weeping in solemn celebration. That same year, the Potter's House received more publicity for the licensing of its treatment center for substance abusers, and Jakes' Woman Thou Art Loosed conference continued to pick up steam and drew 22,000 women to Florida. No preacher had ever capitalized more from a title than Jakes with a Sunday School lesson, a break-through sermon, a popular book that was exceeding a million in sales, a successful yearly conference; and in 1997 Jakes used the "Woman Thou Art Loosed" title once again for his first music CD.

In 1998 Jakes and his ministry showed no signs of losing momentum. He drew 15,000 men to Manpower in Birmingham and 53,000 women to Woman Thou Art Loosed in Atlanta. Jakes also received a Dove Award and a Grammy nomination for his music CD. Although he did not win the Grammy, attending the ceremony gave him a chance to bask in his newfound celebrity as he and Serita exited their limo and made their entrance amid the flashing cameras:

> I will never forget watching Bill Gates as he walked right past me, dressed in his distinguished suit and looking quite successful. Then I saw Danny DeVito, an actor I have enjoyed watching on television and in many motion pictures. Boy, I had come along way from where I grew up in the hills of West Virginia. (Jakes 2002:271)

In the same year, Jakes established another for-profit company called Touchdown Concepts to produce theatrical performances and musical projects. But the most significant achievement of

1998 involved an important publishing deal that brought him even more exposure.

By this time, seven of his eighteen books had been National Christian Booksellers Association best-sellers, and he was selling thousands of videotapes each year as well. But Jakes' quest for greatness inspired his desire to "cross over" and reach a larger audience. This craving was actualized in the beginning of 1998 when he signed a seven-figure contract with the Putnam Publishing Group. Jakes discussed this development in a recent sermon called "You Don't Have to Believe in My Dream":

> When the secular publisher came around and negotiated and said that they wanted me to write for them and that they wanted to publish my books, I went to the meeting—I went right to Wall Street—rolled up in a navy-blue suit a white shirt and an ugly tie. I sat right in there, I talked to them for a long time. . . . And I negotiated, "Now you can publish the books but you can't control the message; I've got to be able to say what I want to say in my books and minister the way I want to minister . . ." and then I started signing.

Jakes released his first book with Penguin Putnam, *The Lady, Her Lover, and Her Lord* to coincide with his Woman Thou Art Loosed conference in 1998 and used the name of the book as the theme of the conference. Jakes orchestrated such a strategic practice in the past with the release of his books *Loose That Man and Let Him Go* and *Naked and Not Ashamed.* He would do the same with his books *Maximize the Moment* in 2000 and *God's Leading Lady* in 2002. This "branding" ploy inspired thousands of attendants to purchase his new books after three days of being inundated with the same titles as the conferences' themes.

A large secular publisher provided exciting new possibilities for marketing his work. Putnam set up a rigorous book tour, and for two to three months Jakes traveled six days a week, in a different city every two days, as one of his personal assistants recalled:

The days were pretty full from early morning radio talk shows, all the way to late night talk shows. Christian, secular, all kinds, whatever they could get him on, book signings, major bookstores, so it was a fairly packed schedule. Bishop keeps a rigorous schedule—even on his downtime he puts most people to shame as far as what he accomplishes. (Interview)

Jakes was no longer with small Christian publishers, but now one of the largest publishing companies was navigating his literary efforts. The book tour paid off as *The Lady, Her Lover, and Her Lord* sold more than 300,000 copies in the first hundred days after it was released and then spent four months at the top of *Publishers Weekly*'s Religion Best-Sellers list.

The year 1998 was special for other reasons. The Potter's House received a million-dollar donation from Jakes' protégé Deion Sanders, and Jakes invited Texas governor George W. Bush and Dallas mayor Ron Kirk to attend the Potter's House's groundbreaking for a new building that has a seating capacity for eight thousand. In August 1998, the *Wall Street Journal* portrayed Jakes as a media phenomenon and declared his ministry a holy empire. Jakes appeared on CNN's show *Larry King Live* in September to discuss President Clinton's moral problems after Jakes was invited to a clergy prayer breakfast at the White House. The *New York Times* opened 1999 with an article by Gustav Niebuhr and Laurie Goodstein that listed Jakes as one of five ministers positioned to replace Billy Graham as the country's preeminent preacher. *Publishers Weekly* named *The Lady, Her Lover and Her Lord* as one of the top five nonfiction books of the year.

Jakes stayed busy throughout 1999 by conducting crusades in Africa and participating in the coronation of a tribal chief; producing his second music CD, called *Sacred Love Songs*; keynoting the National Day of Prayer among the nation's most popular religious leaders in Washington, D.C.; and launching a national prison campaign to reach thousands of incarcerated people. Just when you thought that he had exhausted the possible uses of the title "Woman Thou Art Loosed," Jakes' new production company, Touchdown Concepts, produced a play in 1999 by the same name. The play performed in packed houses nationwide and incorporated common themes addressed in Jakes' sermons and books, such as sexual abuse, alcoholism, and addictive relationships. Jakes invited women's-shelter groups as special guests to each play. The ensemble toured almost every major city and carved a niche as a new type of theatrical gospel presentation.

In the summer of 1999, Jakes drew over 85,000 people to his conference in Atlanta. This was a telling sign that he had become the most popular African American spiritual leader in the country. He had accomplished what only Billy Graham was able to do: selling out the Georgia Dome. In addition to the 85,000 people who came from all over the country to attend the three-day conference, thousands of women in prisons and detention centers were able to watch the proceedings through satellite transmissions.

But 1999 was bittersweet for Jakes: his mother Odith died in August after a protracted battle with various illnesses. In her book, Jacqueline Jakes revealed how her mother remained a bulwark of strength in her last waking moments:

> It was after the sixth of her eight brain surgeries that my mother, a seventy-three-year-old, now one-hundred-pound woman whose will remained strong as her body waned in feebleness, sat visibly trembling. My youngest brother, Tom, whose resolve at that moment was giving way, looked at her through tears of frustration and said, "I don't see how you are handling this!" My mother lifted her bald head and reared her shoulders back and said in a hearty voice, "You do what you have to do, and don't you forget it." (J. Jakes 2002:69)

In Odith's last waking moment, Jacqueline's daughter Kelly sensed that her grandmother was about to die and gathered the family around the hospital bed to bid her farewell. Hundreds of pastors and friends traveled to Dallas to support Jakes as he buried the woman who gave him his faith and tenacity. While maintaining a strong public front, Jakes was privately distraught, as his friend Paul Lewis confirmed: "I talked to him the night she died and I tell you, man, I was scared for him. I never heard him so down. But he pulled out of it, man. He loved his mom." This was the second time Jakes had to watch a parent experience a slow and agonizing death. Jakes established several educational programs and a scholarship fund in his mother's memory.

The following year, Jakes refused to let mounting heresy charges by cult watchers like radio host Jerry Buckner, president of Southern Evangelical Seminary Norman Geisler, and Christian broadcaster Hank Hanegraff stifle his progress. His conference Woman Thou Art Loosed 2000 was a success not only for once again drawing tens of thousands to Atlanta, but also for coordinating efforts with health officials to supply mammogram trucks at the conference for breast cancer screening of women without insurance. The conference also provided an economic empowerment seminar keynoted by Jakes and the renowned poet Maya Angelou. In a Public Relations Newswire released by the ministry on July 21, Jakes explained why he added the empowerment component to the conference:

> As increasing numbers of women become heads of households by choice or necessity, we must develop strategies and provide opportunities for them to be educated and empowered to function wisely in business and money management.

That same year Jakes broke his Manpower attendance record by drawing 25,000 men to St. Petersburg, Florida, while thousands of prisoners watched the three-day conference through interactive satellite links. Once again, Jakes strategically selected the conference theme as the name of his new book released in 2000 called *Maximize the Moment*. This was Jakes' third book with Penguin Putnam, and it quickly soared to number 3 on the *New*

York Times Business Best-Sellers List. Jakes was no longer classi-
fied as just a preacher; the success of the book helped him become
a motivational speaker on the national lecture circuit. He
keynoted annual conferences by the National Council of Black
Mayors, National Black Police Association, and the Congressional
Black Caucus as well as speaking at the popular Essence Music
Festival in New Orleans. All of this occurred while he continued
to pastor one of the fastest-growing churches in the country.

The Potter's House membership was approaching 24,000. In
October 2000 it was time for the church to move into the new
eight-thousand-seat building for which ground was broken two
years earlier. The dedication for the new church facility was a big
event in Dallas. Jakes is probably one of only a few people who
could get Vice President Al Gore and the conservative religious
broadcaster Pat Robertson on the same dais as speakers for the
dedication. George W. Bush, Senator Kay Bailey Hutchison, and
Representative Dick Army all sent congratulatory letters. With
the new building, Potter's House members now worshiped in a
technologically advanced facility with hundreds of seats equipped
with computer and power terminals for downloading notes on lap
tops. In the same year Jakes also made trips to preach in England
and Nigeria. The year 2000 closed with a flattering feature article
in *USA Today* declaring Jakes as one of the nation's people to
watch in 2001.

Jakes continued to proclaim a message of economic empowerment and began to advertise his *Maximize the Moment* video series on infomercials in 2001. With this secular video series, Jakes
was joining the ranks of internationally renowned motivational
speakers like Anthony Robbins selling products through infomercials. The year continued to be profitable as he released his third
musical project "The Storm Is Over" through his company Dexterity Sounds. Jakes continued to expand his entrepreneurial empire with laser-point precision by generating his own line of cards
called "Loose Your Spirit—Messages of Faith and Inspiration"
with Mahogany Cards, a division of Hallmark that targets African

Americans. Like Penguin Putnam, Hallmark was banking on Jakes' secular appeal.

The media continued to be enthralled with Jakes in 2001. The *Washington Post* used over five thousand words to profile Jakes as playwright, best-selling author, and pastor of one of the fastest-growing churches in the nation. More impressively, a few months later Jakes joined the ranks of only a few African American preachers to have appeared on the cover of *Time* magazine. During the same week he adorned the magazine's cover, he was invited to the White House to give counsel to President Bush on the September 11 national tragedy, and he appeared on PBS's *Charlie Rose* show later that night to discuss his meeting with Bush. Like Billy Graham, Jakes had become a presidential counselor and had emerged as a national leader. At the end of 2001, both *Time* and CNN gave Jakes the distinction "America's Best Preacher."

By 2002 Jakes had become easily the most industrious spiritual leader in the country. He was a co-host to Lou Rawls' *Miracle of Stars*, a long-standing televised celebrity fund-raiser for the United Negro College Fund, and he turned more heads when *Savoy* magazine named him among the "Top 100 Powers That Be" in America. He also received another Grammy nomination, an NAACP Image Award, and a Stellar Gospel Award for his gospel music project "The Storm Is Over." But while Jakes was publicly advising women to create a godly and successful legacy, he privately learned that his fourteen-year-old daughter was pregnant with his first grandchild. Jakes, who had spent much time and energy mending families and healing wounds, was left questioning where he went wrong as spiritual leader and father to his teenage daughter.

Although he would later proudly display his grandson Malachi before his church, Jakes made diligent attempts to conceal the pregnancy and birth from the media. The disclosure might have caused damage to his ministry if unforgiving critics learned that the man who leads millions of women to spiritual and psychological wellness could not steer his young daughter from the pitfall of teenage pregnancy. A local journalist broke the story of the pregnancy after rummaging through Jakes' trash and discovering her medical records. After being hounded by several reporters he began closing himself off from the media.

In June 2003, President Bush invited twenty prominent African American preachers to the White House for a private summit. This meeting had the explicit agenda of urban planning and discussing faith-based initiatives, and the implicit function of garnering early support among prominent black clergy for Bush's presidential run in 2004. Anthony Evans, a popular Dallas pastor and radio personality; Kirbyjon Caldwell, a Houston pastor and longtime friend of Bush; and Jakes held prominent seats next to President Bush. While Evans and Caldwell indulged the president, it was Jakes who posed the hard questions and asked about Bush's engagement with African American churches. Mark Scott, an attendee at the meeting, noted:

> Jakes is extremely talented. He walked right into that room and sized it up and quickly emerged as the point man. Some of the other ministers were overwhelmed, excited, unsophisticated, and just happy to be there, but Jakes held his own. Tony and Kirbyjon were pandering to the president with "We're your boys, you know we got your back" kind of annotations, but Jakes was assertive in cautioning the president against patronizing powerful African Americans who can lead their own people and write their own grants. (Interview)

Jakes' poise and authority at the White House showed he had come a long way from his humble days of preaching in coal-mining towns.

Having already experienced tremendous success as a nonfiction author, Jakes decided to release his first novel *Cover Girls* in July 2003. The novel's characters wrestled with the same themes that distinguish his ministry, including emotional and sexual abuse,

discarding dead-weight relationships, standing up to power structures, and tearing down facades. The novel was cathartic for Jakes
because one of the characters had to contend with the shame of
her thirteen-year-old grandchild's pregnancy. The novel vicariously expressed his own fears and emotions about becoming a
grandfather much earlier than he had planned.

Jakes ended 2003 by drawing thousands to his Caribbean
cruise and releasing a book of Christmas stories called *Follow the
Star*. The Potter's House decided to show its appreciation to
members by giving Christmas gifts to everyone in attendance.
One delighted member recalled, "I had never in my life gone to a
Sunday service and received a gift from a church." The year was
also special for Jakes because his church made its last payment on
the building for which ground was broken only a few years earlier.
Jakes' aggressive fund-raising efforts and members' sacrificial support generated enough money to pay off a $35 million mortgage
in only three years. On the last day of 2003, Jakes conducted an
outdoor ceremony to celebrate paying off the debt by burning
the mortgage note in a bonfire. Overwhelmed by the congregation's accomplishment, he repeatedly asked his members, "Is this
a dream?"

The success of *Cover Girls* sparked Jakes' decision to produce
another theatrical production based on the novel. His play *Cover
Girls*, starring the famous television actor Kim Fields, began a nationwide tour in January to a sold-out theater in Dallas, but it was
not quite as successful nationwide. The play had to cancel performances in most cities for not selling enough tickets. Jakes' fail-
ure to duplicate the success of his previous plays sparked one staff
member to ponder if Jakes' influence was in decline. In the
spring, Jakes held his Leadership Summit in London, then had a
two-day crusade in Portland, Oregon, at Memorial Coliseum.

With conference attendance slightly down the last two years,
Jakes responded with his newest effort in June called Mega Fest
2004, a four-day family-vacation event in Atlanta that combined
Manpower and Woman Thou Art Loosed with concerts, preach-

ing, workshops, and fun activities for men, women, college students, and children. Lawrence Robinson, an assistant pastor at the Potter's House claimed Mega Fest drew over 150,000 people, while more conservative estimates suggest no more than 130,000. Mega Fest featured a comedy performance by Steve Harvey, a celebrity basketball game with Magic Johnson, and a concert by pop music star India Arie. Also performing were popular preachers like Paula White, Eddie Long, Creflo Dollar, Juanita Bynum, and Joyce Meyer. By combining preaching, fashion shows, business seminars, sports, music concerts, and so on, Mega Fest reflects the type of postmodern ingenuity that helped Jakes become one of the nation's most influential spiritual leaders. Jakes' uncanny ability to blend the spiritual with the secular is one of the significant traits of his ministry.

Jakes spent much of the summer of 2004 promoting his latest best-seller, *He-Motions: Even Strong Men Struggled.* He conducted public therapy sessions in large churches and conference centers nationwide, discussing themes from the book and encouraging men to become more in touch with their emotions. Inspired by Mel Gibson's successful movie *The Passion of the Christ*, Jakes told a group of pastors in July that the next frontier of evangelism may be the movie theater. In October Jakes made his screen debut in his own R-rated movie called *Woman, Thou Art Loosed*, a fictional account that addresses themes such as sexual abuse and addiction also discussed in the book. The *Los Angeles Times* was among several media outlets that praised Jakes' performance as a compassionate preacher contemplating the vicissitudes of personal tragedy. Jakes' movie was an attempt to reach the sight-and-sound generation and to deal with contemporary problems and struggles. It added another phase to his media empire and confirmed that Jakes is the model of the new postmodern, business-savvy multidimensional preacher.

Jakes' childhood experiences and early years in ministry helped nurture the type of postmodern features that helped him take advantage of a national platform he received after his big break in

1993. He employed shrewd marketing techniques and calculated decisions to increase his momentum and attain a predominant position in American Protestantism. Several preachers received national attention on television, but few applied the organizational savvy and use of mass media to market themselves. Early on, he organized local pastors from various cities to help him draw large crowds and minister to the people and made the names of his sermons and books known through repetition and branding. Establishing popular conferences for men and women was an important decision that made Jakes more than just a preacher but also a power broker similar to his trailblazer, Carlton Pearson. Starting for-profit companies allowed him to control the commercialization of his message and ministry and build a multi-million dollar entrepreneurial empire.

After moving his ministry to Dallas, Jakes built what became one of the largest churches in the country. He is the poster child for a new breed of postmodern preaching superstars who have gained unprecedented wealth and influence through television exposure. Jakes' popularity was the product of a faith industry of neo-Pentecostal broadcast networks, Christian magazines, cyberspace, and eventually secular media. This success demonstrates how spiritual celebrities are hyped in our postmodern technological age and how religion is also affected by vast cultural and technological changes. With best-selling books, videos, theatrical productions, CDs, popular conferences, and Hallmark cards, Jakes explored creative ways to carve out a new market share and commercialize his name and faith. The fact that the secular mass media began to cover him was no ploy to choose black leaders, as some skeptics carped, but was the timely reporting of a phenomenon generating mass appeal since his big break in 1992.

During his rapid rise to fame, Jakes learned how easy it is to suffer from vertigo because air is thinnest at the top. He currently struggles not to lose his equilibrium while grappling with the challenges of stardom. Jakes is often stalked by reporters, receives four to five scathing death threats each week, and has become

suspicious of almost every encounter because of the constant so-
licitations of his name, money, and fame by so-called friends.
Whether it is critics denouncing his flamboyance or theologians
challenging his view of the Trinity, Jakes faces persistent re-
minders that celebrity is coterminous with public scrutiny and
that the great cost of fame is one's privacy.

Jakes' hard work and determination, strategic use of television,
and willingness to take risks such as moving his ministry to Dallas
and starting various business ventures demonstrated the kind of
frontier spirit that characterizes the romantic quest of the American dream. Jakes is an American phenomenon because he blends
postmodern spirituality with the sense of industry exhibited by
business tycoons like Donald Trump and Michael Dell. Jakes'
ability to reinvent himself as a cosmopolitan neo-Pentecostal superstar and his willingness to adjust his methods and procedures
to new environs, new challenges, and new spheres of influence
demonstrate the improvisational nature of the American spirit.
His commercialization of his spiritual gifts to acquire million-dollar homes, luxury cars, fancy Italian suits, and a personal fortune
bordering on $100 million exemplifies the Americanisms of
brazen consumerism and conspicuous consumption.

[4]

A Virtuoso, a Prodigy

Jakes' Appeal in the Spiritual Marketplace

He is a virtuoso, a prodigy. The only thing more exhilarating
than the style of T.D. Jakes' sermons is their rigor and compassion.   —David Van Biema

To some degree we all function like economists. While most of us
do not construct intricate demand curves every time we go shop-
ping, we have a lifetime of practice meeting self-interest. Vendors
pull us in many directions to consume products and services, and
our limited time and resources force us to mull over what to purchase and what to reject. Opting to buy Nas' or Guerilla Black's
new hip-hop CD may force a teenager to forgo seeing the latest
movie if his weekly allowance cannot afford both. Similarly, deciding to attend one of T.D. Jakes' conferences in June may cause
a Baptist woman to miss her denomination's national convention
in September due to limited finances and vacation time.

Scholars of religion are taking note that people make religious
choices by using a similar cost-benefit analysis they use to evaluate
other objects of choice such as employment, housing, and leisure
goods. Like its commercial counterparts, religion functions in a
market of customers along with firms seeking to serve that market
(Finke and Stark 1992). Some clients want theological messages
that rely on a refined and rational theology while others seek spiritual teachings that appeal to emotions and experience (Finke
1997). Some clients seek churches that provide a family atmos-

phere, while others want anonymity. In a competitive and pluralistic American religious economy, churches have to attract, retain, motivate, reward, and satisfy people or face declines in membership.

Rather than dismissing religious choices as irrational or foolish, sociologists advocate a new paradigm to study the success and failures of spiritual institutions at drawing members. This approach emphasizes that the religious marketplace is similar to other economic markets: the spiritual institutions that develop a niche will prosper while those that fail to appeal successfully to some segment of the religious market will slide into oblivion.

> Some readers may shudder at the use of "market" terminology in discussions of religion. But we see nothing inappropriate in acknowledging that where religious affiliation is a matter of choice, religious organizations must compete for members and that the invisible hand of marketplace is as unforgiving of ineffective religious firms as it is of their commercial counterparts. (Finke and Stark 1992:17)

A market approach to religion explores why some congregations and denominations decline in membership while others prosper.

Jakes' ability to provide spiritual commodities that resonate with the pluralistic postmodern tastes of his American listeners distinguishes his thriving ministry. Preachers like Jakes who construct innovative messages toward the existential needs and cultural tastes of many people continue to draw an unprecedented number of followers, while more traditional mainline preachers continue to lose their cherished positions in the marketplace. Jakes secures a loyal following by preaching sermons that answer many of life's questions, writing books and plays that tackle many of life's problems, and producing songs that soothe many of life's pains. He alternates as motivational speaker, psychologist, dietician, financial consultant, entertainer, father figure, and spiritual leader to address many needs. He has been unafraid to step outside the box of traditional Protestantism, and his unique message and virtuosity with American culture contributes to his magnetism and charm. Many important features contribute to Jakes' vast appeal.

Theatrics and Passion

Entertainers who seize the attention of large crowds understand the importance of performance art. Rap star L.L. Cool J craftily licks his lips and moves his body to push the emotional buttons of thousands of women at his concerts, and the R&B diva Mya knows just the right movements to enthrall her male fans. Similarly, Jakes mesmerizes his audiences through the performance art of preaching. "I have never seen Bishop Jakes look down at his notes once," claimed a member of the Potter's House. Jakes raises and lowers his voice, varies his tempo, smiles, dances, or slowly wipes the sweat from his forehead in a manner that creates drama and excitement. Jakes is a master storyteller, creating the feeling that he is speaking directly to each person in his audience, rushing back and forth across the stage with the verve and passion reminiscent of a flamenco dancer. Some may call this God's anointing, others may acknowledge it as the preacher's craft; but either way you frame it, Jakes radiates the kind of energy that leaves audiences spellbound.

In a postmodern media age that pays a high premium on style and simulation, Jakes captivates audiences with riveting sermons, flashy attire, poignant dramatizations, and visual demonstrations to depict key points in his sermons. For example, during a recent sermon series on racism, Jakes created a powerful effect by placing people dressed up as antebellum slaves on stage in chains. Similarly, during one of his Manpower conferences, he had Nautilus weight-lifting equipment placed strategically on stage. A man working out while Jakes was preaching, providing visualization for spiritual growth and development. Another creative tactic Jakes often employs during his sermons is to speak in the place of those hurting and longing for relief. At Woman Thou Art Loosed 1999, Jakes offered such a soliloquy with music playing softly in the background to increase its dramatic effect:

> Oh, will you love me. I have some issues. Love me, hold me, if it's just for the night, hold me. If I can't have a man I'll borrow one. If I can't get a man I'll get a woman. I've just got some issues. I was broken when I was a child and I've got some issues. And anybody that will show me some attention, I'll do anything, just hold me. You don't have to love me, just act like you love me. Just whisper in my ear—I know you're a liar but just tell me that you love me. Hold me for a little while because I'm leaking issues. Buy something every now and then, make me feel special, just tell me you're going to leave her, you don't have to leave her just tell me that you're thinking about leaving her. Tell me you'd leave her if you could. Tell me that you love me.

As Jakes continued to speak as the archetypical hurting woman, the Georgia Dome was filled with thousands of weeping women, indicating he was striking a chord.

Another aspect of Jakes' theatrics and passion involves his use of sensuality. For example, at Woman Thou Art Loosed 2002, Jakes proclaimed that sex is the opiate of creation and urged his listeners not to obscure biblical references to sensuality:

> *The Song of Solomon* has been spiritualized often before we take it literally. I think we do an injustice to the text when we spiritualize it before we take it literally—it is a book about love, about intimacy. It sounds sensual because it is, it simply is. It sounds sexual because it is, and if you would take your religious glasses off for a moment and read *The Song of Solomon* it would make you blush.

Jakes offers tantalizing discussions on love and sensuality that rival Harlequin romance novels. An example is this exhortation in one of his early books for husbands to rekindle the fire in their marriages:

> Have you touched your wife and fondled her, have you toyed with her and played with her, while failing to know her? . . . Roll up your sleeves and reclaim your creativity. Recall the soft songs, light those fragrant candles, take those long walks of longing, and once again murmur passionate words in your mate's ear. (Jakes 1996c:125–126)

Jakes knows that sex sells even in Christendom. He made a fortune on his CD *Sacred Love Songs*, a compilation of romantic songs with smooth and sexy rhythm tracks for Christian couples. Jakes encourages Christians to transfer romantic energy to their worship experience and he conveys a personal God who desires a passionate love affair with humans:

> The Lord wants to make sweet love to you. I'm not being carnal, I'm being real. He wants to hold you. He wants you to come in at the end of the day and say, "Oh, Lord, I could hardly make it today." (Jakes 1997[1993]:95)

Because many churches eschew sexual talk, Jakes profits from an untapped market of Christians who are hungry to explore and appraise sexual energy in a godly context.

Versatility and Creativity

By learning how to exploit new applications from earlier successes, Jakes has been versatile enough to extend his market share. A telling example involves his Mega Fest 2004, an intriguing three-day family-vacation event that drew thousands of people from different denominations and perspectives to pray and play together. Mega Fest included intense worship services, educational forums, business seminars, and entertainment such as fashion shows and a music concert with celebrities. The multidimensional component of this event reflects Jakes' ability to blur traditional lines of distinction between the secular and the spiritual.

Another example of Jakes' ingenuity involves his decision to reinvent a struggling genre by producing black theatrical productions known as gospel plays. Traditionally, gospel plays have been denounced as lowbrow "Chitlin Circuit" shows that lack depth and reinforce black stereotypes. However, Jakes' gospel plays feature complex characters who wrestle with the existential struggles addressed in his sermons and books. Jakes' latest production, *Cover Girls*, based on his best-selling novel, featured television star Kim Fields and the legendary gospel singer Ann Nesby. Jakes chose Mathew Knowles, CEO of Music World Entertainment, as executive producer to ensure a level of professionalism that rivals Broadway plays. Like African American playwright Tyler Perry, Jakes has made millions by improving a genre that combines complex emotional struggles with subtle Christian themes.

Another facet of Jakes' versatility involves his dexterity with touchstones from American culture. He brashly incorporates themes from Hollywood, MTV, or the latest hip-hop video and borrows elements from a number of traditions in interesting and novel ways. His sermons and books sprinkle the individualism of Benjamin Franklin, the pop-psychology of Dr. Phil and Oprah Winfrey, the self-help expertise of Anthony Robbins and Deepak Chopra, and Grandma's good old-fashioned folk wisdom to form a profoundly American and yet highly spiritual message and ministry. For example, in one of his sermons, Jakes recited a large passage of scripture from memory and a few minutes later he shouted, "Y'all gonna make me lose my mind, up in here, up in here," as a playful reference to the hook of a hit song by rapper DMX. In his novel *Cover Girls*, Jakes quotes everyone from writer John Steinbeck to pop singer Mary J. Blige. A critic once gave Jakes the pejorative moniker the "Velcro Bishop" because pop culture references "stick" to him.

Jakes' intellectual prowess contributes to his versatility as well. Even though he is a sharp thinker, he never comes across as cerebral. Harold Dean Trulear Jr., a noted sociologist of religion, once carpooled with Jakes and marveled at his trenchant analysis of psychological theories regarding race:

> I was in the limousine going to the hotel to the consecration service with Bishop T.D. Jakes, Bishop Eric Garnes, and Bishop Mears. Bishop Garnes and Bishop Jakes got into a discussion of the psychology that fit into their theological understandings of what was going on among black people in general and black families and women in particular, and they entered into this major discussion of the Isis Papers. It was very clear that these were very well read men and they weren't just accepting what Dr. Frances Cress Welsing said without criticism; they were engaging the whole thesis that black people by virtue of oppression have come to a certain kind of psychological status and that the church had to deal with the pain and the suffering that black people had encountered by virtue of their journey in this country. Jakes was affirming that there was a dimension to Welsing's diagnosis that had to be addressed. (Interview)

Donald Hilliard, a prominent pastor in New Jersey, speculates that Jakes has a photographic memory and marvels at his intellect. Religion scholar Leonard Lovett is equally impressed by Jakes' aptitude:

> Jakes is not well educated, but he's intelligent. Now, anybody who confronts Jakes and doesn't admit that has got to be crazy. He's highly intelligent. He's the kind of guy that if he had been educated, he might have been dangerous. (Interview)

Jakes demonstrates a broad knowledge of world affairs and preaches like a contemporary Renaissance man.

Another important aspect of Jakes' versatility involves his desire to blur the traditional lines of distinction concerning race.

"When I looked all around Reliant Stadium I saw thousands of black, white, Asian, and Hispanic women," recalled Pat Murphy after attending Woman Thou Art Loosed 2003 in Houston. Although Jakes' style and magnetism resembles traits nurtured in the black church experience, his message is racially neutral. Jakes has shown versatility by preaching beyond the walls of the black church and has been featured in diverse contexts, including keynoting rallies for Promise Keepers in the mid-1990s, Pat Robertson's tent revivals, and various other platforms generally closed to black preachers. In his last years in West Virginia, Jakes' church peaked with 35 percent white membership, and the Potter's House has maintained a strong interracial and multiethnic following. He has made numerous public statements urging black and white Christians to get out of their racial comfort zones. Jakes' conferences and video sales reflect his growing interracial following, giving credence to *Time* magazine's claim that he has become America's preacher.

Transformative Message

"He's not like any other minister that I know because he deals so much with psychology and inner healing," declared John Jacobs who twice attended Manpower and often purchases Jakes' sermon videos. Another feature behind Jakes' mass appeal involves an ability to address human concerns like an existentialist philosopher. His experience as a psychology major provided a healthy respect for the human condition and psychological savvy for solving complex problems. As a young Pentecostal preacher, Jakes already knew about spiritual deliverance, but studying psychology taught him that the fundamental problems humans face are both psychological and spiritual. Consequently, Jakes became a postmodern preacher seeking to combine godly wisdom with insight on the human condition. Whether he is delineating the struggles of a single mother raising her family or addressing the frustrations of middle-aged men, Jakes maneuvers a mélange of psychology and scripture to diagnose human crises.

"Bishop Jakes preaches his own struggles and his message is very touchable," asserted George Wilson, a frequent attendee at Manpower. In an interview, Nailah Harris, a longtime follower of Jakes from Staten Island, discussed her experience at Woman Thou Art Loosed:

> I was dealing with depression, my emotions, and stress and so I needed to get away. What I got out of the conference was restoration and added strength to move on with my life. Bishop Jakes helped me realize I had to manage my emotions, trust the Lord for my future, and practice forgiveness with reconciliation. (Interview)

Jakes addresses the emotional disabilities and imperfections that preachers often gloss over, while also emphasizing God's ability to heal and change situations. Jakes' childhood struggles with fear and low self-esteem, his father's slow and agonizing death, combined with his toil in abject poverty during early years in ministry generated a soft spot for people experiencing pain and emotional turmoil. He goes beyond identifying pain to form a teleological appropriation of it, or more simply put, he imputes God's greater purpose to one's hurts and struggles. Jakes argues that pain is a good sign that God is about to birth greatness in a person's life:

> If you have been in pain, maybe it is because the baby is coming. The baby is the destiny that God is birthing in your life, and the pain is a sure indication that you are getting close to your delivery. There is no time to faint now, dear lady. Grab the sides of the bed and push! (Jakes 1998:75–76)

Unlike philosophers like Arthur Schopenhauer and Jean-Paul Sartre who bewailed the absurdity and randomness of human suffering, Jakes assures his audience that God has a purpose for all believers and chooses to use pain and struggle to prepare them. Jakes teaches that suffering should not dehumanize and that Christians should link their current pain with God's anointing on their lives.

Along with his appropriation of pain, Jakes is a master at creating teleological expectation, or the belief that God's future blessing awaits faithful believers. Jakes tells his listeners that nothing in their past can hold them from a blessed future if they make up their minds and go forward. In 2002 at Manpower, Jakes urged his male audience to act like men on a specific mission from God:

> Life is asking you a question: What did you come down here to do? Why are you on the planet? You cannot spend the next ten, twenty, thirty years joyriding through life trying to see what happens; looking for the next thrill, the next game, the next opportunity. You have to identify yourself as being a man on a mission. That means, "I'm not a mistake. I'm not an accident. I'm not just the end result of a man and woman that got together and copulated their way into my existence. I'm not something that just wandered onto the stage of life"—God has a plan for your existence.

Akin to how Oral Roberts utilized his popular saying, "Something good is going to happen to you," Jakes has become famous for his "Get ready, get ready, get ready" catch phrase that motivates his audience to prepare for a future with limitless possibilities. Jakes appeals to multitudes of desperate people longing for a glimmer of hope and offers solace for people in pain.

Like many postmodern preachers, Jakes has made peace with complexity. He has a penchant for interweaving conflicting theological traditions: one that emphasizes free will and human agency and another that focuses on God's control over all events. Jakes' message of agency exhorts his followers to develop life plans and take advantage of every moment. He places the responsibility on the believer to fulfill his or her potential by practicing good habits and learning important principles. This emphasis on agency is captured in an excerpt from his *Maximize the Moment* video series:

> God is not a respecter of persons but he is a respecter of principles, and if you don't learn the principles you will never get the product. It has nothing to do with who you are as a person. It has something to do with principles. Understanding those principles, moving into those principles, and by living by those principles has all to do with how well you do in school, how well you do in college, how well you do in corporate, how well you do in kingdom—it makes no difference what you are aspiring to, your success is predicated on you understanding and learning the principles.

In contrast to his emphasis on human agency, Jakes often places success out of the believer's control and into God's hands as part of God's incontrovertible plan and purpose, as a passage from one of his books demonstrates:

> Eventually all the seemingly terrible events of your life will fit into the scheme of God's divine omniscient plan. When He unveils the completed picture, it will appear, not as a canvas of confusion, but as a perfect portrait of his love for you. (Jakes 1996b:32)

Such an intriguing dance between conflicting themes of God's sovereignty and human agency is useful because Jakes can reassure his followers that their steps are ordered by God, while at the same time encourage them to aggressively pursue their destiny. As a postmodern preacher, Jakes does not have to delineate the implications of maintaining theological perspectives in tension. He draws from both traditions even when discussing his rise to fame: on the one hand, he argues that God predestined his worldwide ministry and opened strategic doors that no human could have closed; but on the other hand, he acknowledges that his own tenacity, dedication, and sacrifice shaped his destiny. Jakes intertwines God's supernatural intervention with human responsibility. The result is a profoundly spiritual and acutely human message of uplift.

"I love my pastor because he lets the people know, 'I'm Bishop Jakes but I go through things too.' He's just all about being real," noted a young adult female attendee of his church. Another facet of Jakes' transformative message involves his iconoclastic vision of eradicating what he perceives to be hypocrisy from the church. Jakes argues that for too long the church has neglected the human side of Christianity, that is, vulnerability and imperfection:

> When we hide, we turn phony. We act out a charade. We put on a "face" and participate in our own masquerade. Only two things are worse than being phony with other people: being phony with yourself, and being phony with God. (Jakes 1997a:81)

A recurring theme in many of Jakes' sermons and books is that the church should be a safe haven where Christians can be honest and transparent. Jakes' recent movie *Woman Thou Art Loosed* dramatized the common, and yet tragic, practice of covering up serious issues of sexual abuse with facades of spirituality. Jakes strongly asserts that the church has been guilty of focusing too much on Christian ideals rather than addressing the realities of contemporary times. His iconoclastic ministry strikes a chord with thousands of Christians who have been alienated by religious hypocrisy or frustrated by the pressure to put on holy masks:

> We have hidden our humanity beneath the man-made cloths of religiosity. We have covered up what God has made bare! Now we have to face secular news reporters who are trying to expose what should have been uncovered from the beginning. (Jakes 1997a:16)

Although some typecast Jakes as a preacher for women, Jakes' transformative message is quite popular among men as well. "No one in the activist community has been nearly as successful getting men to deal with inner wounds and imperfection as Jakes," claimed Hitaji Aziz, a popular radio personality and activist. Aziz recalled one of Jakes' meetings in which hundreds of men who suffered from past sexual abuse came to the altar crying and seeking healing. Rodney Sadler also commented on Jakes' uncanny ability to draw men together and transform their lives:

> I attended one of his conferences a few years back just to see what was going on and was very impressed by the fact that he had gotten black men from across the country to come together and love each other. I spent a good time in Washington, D.C. and I know how African American men usually related in that city but for the time period of Jake's Manpower Conference meetings men were walking around the streets hugging each other where they usually grit on each other so it was a remarkable transformation and I have to give him kudos for being able to make us more self-aware and appreciate ourselves as being made in God's image. (Interview)

Jakes' latest best-seller, *He-Motions: Even Strong Men Struggle*, encourages men to discard macho stereotypes, understand their emotions, and control their struggles with power, money, and sex.

Jakes preaches to those individuals who find themselves in their second or third marriage, because he knows that "happily ever after" is found in children's storybooks, not in many homes. He convinces his listeners that they may be broken and wounded, they may be raising their children alone, they may be backed in a corner, but their lives are still meaningful and hopeful. His compassion for the underdog motivates his national prison ministry, which broadcasts his conferences and church services through interactive satellites to thousands in prisons nationwide. Jakes often prescribes hope for people who experienced sexual and emotional abuse, drug addiction, poverty, and little education. He emphasizes that God gives second chances and new beginnings and that God's greatness is often fertilized by human weakness.

Jakes identifies with people who are at their lowest moment by extracting from his personal experience. He frequently alludes to the rough times when he had to dig ditches to feed his family, and when his wife and kids had to share a hot dog and can of beans for dinner. Jakes gives hope by conveying that God is about to do a new thing in their lives and that their current struggle is a platform for God's power. He preaches a simple message that you can become healthy and whole through a transformative relationship with God. By creating an atmosphere where all people can feel relevant to God's kingdom, Jakes crafts an appealing message to people previously neglected in spiritual institutions.

Sociologists are embracing a new paradigm that studies spiritual institutions as firms competing to offer religious products for potential clients. This economic approach assumes that forces of supply and demand influence religious choices like commercial ones, and that religious suppliers seek to be unique in ways that are widely valued by their clients. Jakes demonstrates that pastors who arm themselves with an expansive cultural repertoire for solving practical life problems relating to finances, weight loss, self-esteem, and so on, will draw many customers, while one-dimensional ministries may continue to lose market share. To sum it up in economic language, religious suppliers like Jakes who package and promote their religious products toward the existential needs and cultural tastes of their clients attain greater market share than those who do not.

Jakes' appeal comes from a variety of sources: his ability to incorporate touchstones from American culture; his message to the downcast and disenfranchised; and his knack for addressing problems ignored by other preachers, such as sexual abuse and abandonment. Jakes draws from past experiences with family tragedy, poverty, and feelings of inadequacy to diagnose people's struggles and pain. As an iconoclast, Jakes confronts Christian hypocrisy and urges believers to be transparent before God. He employs psychological savvy, business acumen, and an arsenal of scriptures to generate expectancy and bring hope with a message of prosperity.

[5]

A Message of Prosperity

My job as a theologian is to tell Fred Price and T.D. Jakes
that they cannot really be true to the gospel of Jesus if they
preach a message of prosperity that contradicts it. I would say
what they are preaching is very interesting and meaningful to
the people at some other level, but it is not meaningful at the
true gospel level.   —James Cone

There was a time when being Pentecostal meant eschewing the
material blessings of the world by opting for a life of simplicity
not unlike what Henry David Thoreau endorsed in his classic
book *Walden*. Carlis Moody, a longtime bishop in the Church of
God in Christ, recalled the days when Pentecostal and poor were
almost synonymous:

> See, in the early times fifty years ago, much of the folk who were in
> the Pentecostal church were poor. They heard the Word of God
> gladly because it gave them hope for a better way, for a better day
> and they were looking forward to meeting Jesus. (Interview)

Whether it was motivated by sour grapes or otherworldly theology, black Pentecostals of the early and middle twentieth century
shunned lavish living as worldliness that brought enmity from
God. Even when Pentecostal pastors began to prosper beyond
the socioeconomic echelons of their congregants, their avarice
was rarely flaunted or swanked behind the pulpit. But with the
contemporary influx of young, upwardly mobile, middle-class

neo-Pentecostals, all this would change, as Ernestine Reems noted:

> Years ago nobody had money and nobody could do what we're doing. My daddy went through pure hell, but I don't have to go through that now because my church says, "Well, Pastor Reems, we want you to have the best drop-top Mercedes they make." That's the generation of people I pastor; they want you to have the best, they love to see you dress the best, and they want you to live in the best houses. Thirty years ago they were jealous and evil, wouldn't give you any money. (Interview)

Few neo-Pentecostals born after 1980 could possibly conceive the church world in which their grandparents grew up.

The late Kenneth Hagin Sr. was the pioneer of a small group of white ministers called "word of faith" teachers who, by the 1960s, began to challenge healing evangelists as leaders of the neo-Pentecostal movement. Their attempt was to provide a deeper understanding of the rightful place of Christians in God's kingdom, which included financial prosperity and perpetual health and well-being for all believers who learned how to use their faith and positive confessions correctly. Hagin, who preached over the radio and wrote books in the 1960s, formulated a worldview that gave Christians total control over their fates and destinies. In the early 1970s, he started a Bible institute in Oklahoma that trained ministers in this new way of faith and helped the movement grow dramatically a decade later.

Word-of-faith teaching asserts that Christians have the power to control their physical well-being and financial fortunes through their faith. The underlying assumption is that the death and resurrection of Jesus Christ provided Christians with the ability to live in total victory, financial prosperity, and perfect health. However, God's "hands are tied" from blessing many Christians who lack faith and misappropriate biblical principles, thus explaining why all Christians are not experiencing prosperous and healthy lives. Word-of-faith preachers argue that once believers strengthen their faith by memorizing and confessing scriptures, they are able to live in total victory and control their physical and financial fate. The prosperity gospel is a central part of word-of-faith teachings and suggests God wants all believers to prosper financially and will bless them according to their faith.

The timely spread of the prosperity gospel in the 1980s resonated with millions of Americans already hypnotized by the burgeoning consumer culture of the Reagan era and the explosion of wealth inflamed by the rise of Wall Street, producing unprecedented financial prosperity. The rapid rise of blacks to the middle and upper classes in the 1980s happened so suddenly that they were not socialized by the rigid cultural blueprint of the black aristocracy that had been in place, prescribing Catholic, Presbyterian, or Episcopalian churches for social cachet and networking opportunities. As a result, almost every city nationwide has at least one black neo-Pentecostal mega church where middle-class and wealthy African Americans worship, network, and put their skills and talents to use. Prosperity teachings allow them to enjoy their wealth and consumerism as their rightful inheritance as God's faithful children.

White neo-Pentecostalism gained visibility through national figures such as Oral Roberts and Kathryn Kuhlman, and black neo-Pentecostalism procured a facelift through business-savvy prosperity preachers like Creflo Dollar, I.V. Hilliard, and T.D. Jakes. These preachers have national television ministries and are not shy about their million-dollar personal portfolios and lavish lifestyles. No one played a more prominent role in promoting the discourse of prosperity as the groundwork for this new age of millionaire black neo-Pentecostalism than Frederick K.C. Price. As a pioneer of this new movement, Fred Price is one of the most important African American preachers of the twentieth century.

The Godfather of Faith

In 1953, shortly after finishing high school and marrying his wife Betty, Fred Price converted to Christianity. Only a month later, through an unusual experience, he felt that God called him to the ministry:

> I had a divine encounter in the sense that I heard what to me was the voice of God speaking to me very audibly, just as audibly as I'm talking to you right now, and yet no one else in the building heard the voice and it was very plain to me, and the voice simply said, "You are to speak my gospel." (Interview)

For the next seventeen years of his life, Price matriculated through Baptist, African Methodist Episcopal, Presbyterian, and Christian Missionary Alliance churches. Finally he became agitated with his Christian experience. His frustration with the emotionalism of worship in black churches caused him to sense something was lacking in his spiritual development:

> I wasn't getting information, I was just getting inspiration and it left me with a very empty void on the inside. Finally I became so frustrated with my state at that time, until I got so quiet, I guess, that I began to hear the Lord speaking to me through his word and then put me into contact with a man, Kenneth Hagin, who was a Pentecostal teacher, and his tapes and books were the catalysts off the launching pad of the desert into the heaven, as it were. (Ibid.)

A friend first introduced Fred Price to word-of-faith teachings in 1970 by sharing some of Kenneth Hagin's books, as Price explained:

> At that time there were just small books and there were only 32 pages to each book, but each book had something to do with the

Holy Spirit, with faith, etc. And somehow I went home that night
and read every single book and I was changed forever. It was like
scales came off my eyes and I was able to see truths that I had
never seen before even though I had read the same Bible passages
but they never spoke to me that way. (Ibid.)

Price continued to devour Hagin's teachings and presented them
to his new church, Crenshaw Christian Center in California,
which grew rapidly. Price later became a cherished guest speaker
at Hagin's yearly camp meetings. Many black pastors in California
became disgruntled with Price's prosperity theology and began to
criticize his messages publicly. Yet by 1975, while Crenshaw grew
to a thousand members, Price began to consider how to promote
prosperity teachings through radio and television. During this
time Oral Roberts, Billy Graham, Pat Robertson, Rex Humbard,
Robert Schuller, and several others developed national visibility
through their television ministries. Fred Price and his church began to buy television time to promote his teachings first in Los
Angeles and then in Washington, D.C., Chicago, Detroit, and
New York City before eventually expanding nationwide.

Price's television ministry was important for several reasons.
For one, Price and Kenneth Copeland, a white disciple of Kenneth Hagin, became the first prosperity teachers on national television and therefore played dominant roles in making the beliefs
become a growing part of neo-Pentecostalism. Although Oral
Roberts, Jim Bakker, and other televangelists alluded to material
blessings in the 1970s and 1980s, none did so with the deliber-
ateness, intensity, and frequency as word-of-faith preachers like
Price and Copeland. Price also became one of the first African
American preachers on national television, promoting a new way
to be black and Pentecostal. He consistently chided the emotionalism of the black church and offered a polished lecturing format
as an alternative model for teaching ministries to challenge the
anti-intellectualism that was prevalent in many black Pentecostal
churches (Daniels 2001). Price also boasted on television about

his million-dollar salary and Rolls Royce, and taught that blacks can have their blessings on earth if they confess God's word and walk in faith.

Price earned the nickname "The Godfather of Faith" because of his role as mentor to many word-of-faith African American pastors, who eventually established what are now called "word churches" in cities nationwide that teach the word-of-faith message. Instead of advocating protest marches, voting drives, and other forms of activism familiar to black church movements, word churches teach members that poverty is a curse of the devil and that the power to transform their oppression resides within their ability to appropriate their faith and take their rightful place in the kingdom of God. Prosperity theology's answer to poverty is to teach people to build up their faith and be aware of biblical promises. Such a new worldview was appealing to the growing black middle class and especially attractive to all poverty-stricken minorities stretching for a glimmer of hope.

Sociologist Milmon Harrison contends that the prosperity gospel may be especially appealing to black churches that have had to engage both the material and spiritual needs of their members in their historical struggle with oppression and discrimination (Harrison 2005). Today it would be very difficult to find an African American church with members unaffected by prosperity teachings. Creflo Dollar in Atlanta, Keith Butler in Detroit, Leroy Thompson in Louisiana, Clinton and Sara Utterbach in New York, Bill Winston in Chicago, I.V. Hilliard in Houston, Michael and Dee Dee Freeman in Maryland, Steve Parson in Richmond, and Don Shorter in Tacoma, Washington, have joined Price and a host of African American pastors of mega churches and national ministries who unabashedly teach prosperity and divine health through television, radio broadcasts, and books. Their use of mass media makes it impossible for conventional pastors to shield their members from the attractive teachings that suggest believers can control their financial destiny. Many follow Price's lead by adopting a media-savvy and professional image that resonates with the proliferation of middle-class blacks who are turned off by a perceived lack of decorum in traditional Pentecostal churches (Daniels 2001).

The prosperity movement introduced a new culture of giving which convinces Christians to view their financial support to the church as investment opportunities to "sow" their way out of debt to receive God's bountiful blessings. Under such an ideology, preachers train their members to applaud when it is time to collect offerings because God "loves a cheerful giver." Even among traditional mainliners, it is difficult to find a black church in America without at least some members confessing scriptures to build up their faith, believing that God will provide a supernatural increase in finances, or reading books on prosperity such as *Money, Thou Art Loosed!* by Leroy Thompson, *The Purpose of Prosperity* by Fred Price, and *No More Debt* by Creflo Dollar. Even congregations that do not distinguish themselves as word churches often invite popular prosperity teachers as guest speakers, and many members are affected by these teachings. Consequently, prosperity theology has become an important facet of the black church and American Protestantism.

Prosperity preachers often have adversarial relationships with other pastors in their communities. We can attribute some of this to resentment from pastors who lose members to popular word churches each year. However, much of the antagonism comes from strong disagreement with prosperity theology. For example, T.A. Body, a pastor in Atlanta, believes prosperity teachings are unbiblical and has been using sermons and radio broadcasts to disparage them for decades. Similarly, James Blocker, a prominent New York City pastor and vocal critic of the prosperity gospel, discussed how preachers seduce members to give money to the church:

> Many Christians are seduced into giving by the promise of riches. The Christian is encouraged to plant a seed, make a confession, and expect a hundredfold return on their offerings. The minister is

armed with a myriad of proof texts accompanied by his own rags to riches testimony supporting his claim that the Christian should and will become rich by giving offerings, making their appeal to give finances even harder to resist. Motivated by this, the Christian gives his offering expecting to receive a great financial windfall. (Excerpt from CD)

In his CD *Is Giving to Get Rich Biblical?* Blocker criticizes prosperity preachers for misinterpreting scripture, manipulating congregants with tautologies such as, "If you're not rich then you must not have enough faith," and for offering appeals that are "no different than late-night television infomercial get-rich-quick schemes designed to entice the greed in our fallen nature." Arthur Brazier, the longtime pastor of one of the largest churches in Chicago, also voiced his concern about prosperity preachers:

> It concerns me that so many ministers have made prosperity an ambition as the key point of their ministry, and I think that it neglects the reason for the death, burial, and resurrection of Jesus Christ. I think that they have ignored the essential reason for the existence of the church. The church does not exist for us to make money or to gain power and success. (Interview)

Other pastors, to prove that the nexus of faith and financial prosperity lacks biblical precedence, attack prosperity preaching by reminding their members of the Apostle Peter's statement, "Silver and Gold have I none," and that the Apostle Paul never traveled in golden chariots.

The offensive tone of many prosperity preachers on their television broadcasts produces more contention among local pastors. The preachers often mock traditional black churches publicly for selling chicken dinners to raise money and for overlooking the principles of biblical faith as they see them. Even though Jakes is not as discordant as other prosperity preachers, local black pastors are still hostile toward him. As one of his staff members sarcastically stated, "He's not the most cherished guy in Dallas." At a recent staff meeting, a teary-eyed Jakes questioned why so many pastors in Dallas are attacking his teachings.

Jakes and Prosperity

West Virginia coal-mining towns felt the pervasive influence of the prosperity gospel, and Jakes became an early proponent there. When Jakes made his break from obscurity in the early 1990s, prosperity theology had already taken root in him and in the psyches of Christians nationwide. While quickly growing in fame and exposure after his big break in 1993, Jakes exhibited the kind of lavishness depicted in hip-hop music videos. He used prosperity theology to justify his new cars, multimillion dollar home, expensive suits, and extravagant lifestyle as part of God's wish for all believers. Despite the growing acceptance of prosperity teachings among Christians, the print media were less sympathetic to Jakes' excesses and began to write scathing editorials that eventually led to his move to Dallas.

Jakes' troubles in West Virginia began with a front-page article by Ken Ward Jr. in the *Charleston Gazette* on April 5, 1995. It discussed how Jakes' family moved from their modest home in Cross Lanes to purchase a sixteen-room mansion in St. Albans for $630,000 from local banker George T. Martin. The article disclosed that Jakes also purchased a second smaller house adjacent to the mansion for $240,000, placing the total price of both homes just under a million dollars. The article mentioned the elaborate security system, tall stone fence, swimming pool, and bowling alley inside the new mansion. Jakes said that he was "surprised and affronted" that a reporter would ask about the price of his home, and his defensive response was included in the article:

> Are you saying that it's inappropriate? I don't think it's unusual. I don't think it's excessive. I'm not only a minister. I'm on national

television and I'm the author of five books. If you're successful, it's not unusual to have a nice home. There are many prominent ministers who are successful. I don't think that is necessarily suspicious.

The article sparked a critical response from many Charleston residents, and a series of scathing editorials criticized Jakes' lavish lifestyle. Another article on Jakes appeared in the *Charleston Daily Mail* on April 8 with the headline, "Ministry Not Shy about Collections." This article discussed the Friday night service at Jakes' Back to the Bible Conference and reviewed Jakes' collection of the offering:

> Jakes said later "God opened a window." The window was big enough and open long enough—about a half hour—for hundreds to surge forward to the stage, white offering envelopes in hand. "You better get in it, you better get in, you better get it in," Jakes said as musicians played jazzy songs behind his constant patter and constant movement back and forth across the stage. Jakes paced, danced a step or two and wiped his brow with a handkerchief while he brought in the money, sounding much like an auctioneer. "One hundred dollars $1000; c'mon, c'mon," Jakes said.
>
> "I want $20, $50, $29.99," he said. "That's 22," Jakes said when what he said was the 22nd check for $1000 reached the stage. It joined other envelopes in a pile that kept growing. Then another $1000 contribution came in. "That's 23," he said.
>
> "Don't you give God's money to the mall," he said. And a little later: "Somebody else just went home to get a checkbook." "I don't care if you give $5 or $500,000, as long as you do what God wants you to do," Jakes said toward the end of the midday offering time.

The article also revealed that throughout the conference Jakes linked financial gifts from attendees with rewards that only God's faithful will enjoy.

Two days later, on April 10, the *Charleston Gazette* printed an editorial by Dan Ranmacher with the headline: "Liberal Offerings' Minister Lives Good Life." Ranmacher made a connection between the thousands of attendees who paid forty dollars each to hear Jakes at the conference and Jakes' ability to spend nearly a million dollars on two pieces of real estate:

> If Jakes were a rock singer, no one would find fault with him. But he's a minister, someone whose followers say has been touched by God. His money comes from those same followers, many of whom sacrifice to heed the call of one of Jakes' assistants last week to cough up 'a liberal offering and put it in the hands of God and let him do something for you.' Yeah, something like, "help make Jakes' house payment."

Less than two weeks passed before the *Charleston Gazette* published another scathing editorial on Jakes, with the headline: "TV Preachers Being Called a Bishop Doesn't Mean You Can Live Like a King." The author argued that Jakes' mansion with an indoor swimming pool and bowling alley does not follow the biblical admonition for Christians to live in modesty. The author added:

> The New Testament, the manual by which Christians are supposed to live, is laced with examples of humbleness and righteousness. Love thy neighbor, help the poor, the meek shall inherit the earth. Christians and especially ministers should set an example by this and not live like kings. The love of money is the root of all evil.

Several months later the *Gazette* published the decisive blow that pushed Jakes away to Dallas in 1996. A month after Jakes drew thousands to West Virginia for his self-help conference for pastors, the *Charleston Gazette* published James Toler's anti-Jakes editorial with the scathing headline: "A Huckster Is a Huckster: Preachers' Opulent Living Isn't Christianity." The article compared Jakes to religious hucksters who capitalize on their large followings:

> Jakes seems to think that ministers should not be criticized for living high on the hog. He calls it "occupational discrimination" and hints that there is an air of racial discrimination about it, at least in his case. He told Jackson he could provide a list of "50 prominent ministers" across the country who live in houses similar to his. No doubt they drive expensive cars too. Does that make it right? A huckster is a huckster. It's morally wrong to live a life of luxury off the proceeds of religious followers. It's not what Christianity is about.

Jakes felt betrayed by West Virginians for criticizing his opulent lifestyle and for not appreciating the new exposure and business he was providing with his conferences, which were drawing thousands of tourists. He was defensive about his right to live a prosperous life and insisted it was God's will that all believers flourish financially. Jakes contended that soldiers gambled for Jesus Christ's cloak while he was on the cross, so he must have had great wealth, and therefore Christ's followers should emulate him by being wealthy. Jakes also felt that because he preached as a pauper for so many years, he should not have to apologize for flourishing and teaching prosperity as God's wish for his believers. Bitterness sparked by the derisive articles finally drove Jakes to leave the state.

After relocating to Dallas in 1996, Jakes continued to live first class and purchased a 10,000 square foot mansion for $1.7 million in Lakewood, the wealthy suburbs that housed bankers, athletes, and other members of the Dallas elite. In a *Christianity Today* article two years later, Jakes boasted that he bought the biggest house he could afford because there is nothing wrong with being blessed. His book and video sales continued to grow, and also his style. He had long discarded the tight-fitting iron-shined suits of his past, and by now was clad in designer outfits and Italian suits. Nothing was too good for Serita, either, because she suffered the humble days without complaining. It was her turn to be decked out in fancy dresses and expensive jewelry.

Like most prosperity preachers, Jakes boasts about his material-istic lifestyle and fancy vacations. In a recent sermon, "Provision for the Vision," Jakes bragged about his stable of luxury cars: "We're in a situation now where we've got more cars than we've got garage space to put it." At the end of 2003 Jakes purchased a new Bentley to add to an already impressive vehicle collection that included a Mercedes-Benz, BMW, Lexus as well as a jet. His materialism resembles that of other prosperity preachers like Fred Price, who flies from coast to coast in his Lear jet, and I.V. Hilliard, who wears full-length fur coats, an expensive diamond ring, and flies in his private helicopter to avoid traffic while travel-ing to the churches he pastors in north and southwest Houston. Prosperity preachers flaunt tremendous wealth before their con-gregants as validation of their faith. Fifty years ago, Christians would have viewed Jakes' luxurious lifestyle and excessive materi-alism more circumspectly, but the prosperity movement provided a religious landscape that encouraged more Christians to take a mixture of faith and materialism for granted.

During his dramatic rise to fame in the early 1990s, Jakes quickly shared the dais with prominent prosperity teachers at con-ferences. Today he invites prosperity preachers like Creflo Dollar, Joyce Meyer, and I.V. and Bridget Hilliard to his church and con-ferences and incorporates prosperity theology into his sermons and fund-raising efforts. Here is an excerpt from Jakes' fund-rais-ing letter in 2002, showing a nexus between making a financial contribution to his ministries and God performing a miracle in the giver's life:

> Remember, no need is too big for God. Maybe you need a miracle in your marriage. God can put it back together. You could be fac-ing unbelievable financial challenges; God can provide a supernat-ural increase. God knows where you need your miracle harvest,

and now is the time to sow your Miracle Faith Seed. Even if you've already shared a gift, you still have time to increase your blessing during this miracle season of sowing. Take a moment to do two things: First, write your most urgent prayer request on the reply form and send it to me so I may join you in praying for your miracle harvest! Second, take a moment to sow the most generous miracle faith seed you can.

This excerpt demonstrates a popular principle among word-of-faith teachers called "seed faith." Prosperity preachers claim that by making a contribution to a church or ministry, Christians are planting a "seed" to which God will respond with a supernatural harvest of financial blessings. Jakes explained this "seed-time-and-harvest" principle a month later in another fund-raising letter distributed to supporters:

In order to receive an expected harvest, we must first sow a seed. This positions us to receive or become a reaper. The reaper first receives the blessing of God in the spirit realm. It is conceived by the promises of God's Word becoming a reality in our hearts. This is why getting the Word of God is so important. It is what frames the provision He has for our lives. You can't receive what you can't conceive. Don't ignore the vision God is placing in you now. Recognize the need to sow toward your future. Start now, to prepare not according to your current circumstances but rather in preparation for where you are going. The visions and dreams God has given are a preview to the coming attraction.

Such fund-raising tactics now seem mild compared to other prosperity preachers heard on television and in mega churches nationwide.

Prosperity theology emphasizes that God will open the windows of heaven and pour out a blessing to the faithful Christian who consistently gives money to his local church. This pervasive ideology helps word churches secure more resources while allowing pastors to enjoy large salaries and unprecedented wealth. Like most prosperity preachers, Jakes often encourages members to step out in faith and trust God by giving sacrificially, and that God, in return, will bless them with supernatural debt cancellation and abundant riches. In 1996 Jakes made a request for a thousand members of the Potter's House to step out in faith and give a hundred dollars beyond offering and tithes to help pay off the church's debt. Similarly, in a 2003 service at the Potter's House, he encouraged members to step out in faith and donate a week's salary, as a current member recalled:

> Bishop said God told him to do it and that he was just letting the church know that he was doing the same thing. He told the church to do that and a lot of people came to the front and gave one week of their paycheck. A lot of people were believing God for homes, new cars, and you know the normal things that people believe God for. (Interview)

Jakes' preaching has shifted even more toward prosperity theology in the last few years. He often spends entire sermons inspiring members to give more financial support in order to receive greater blessings from God. It is a common practice at the Potter's House (and in word churches nationwide) for members to rise from their seats, walk down the aisle, and place money on the stage while Jakes is preaching—it is a visible sign of support to their pastor. This helps explain why his church was able to pay off its $35 million mortgage in only three years.

Part of Jakes' appeal involves his ability to amalgamate the quest of the American dream with the Christian experience. In this way Jakes incorporates the prosperity gospel with a profoundly American message of individualism and self-actualization. Jakes contends that God has unlimited blessings for all believers, but adds the caveat that discipline and self-determination are necessary ingredients for believers to be successful. Jakes' spiritual pragmatism teaches that personal faith in God along with practical action will produce prosperity and success in virtually any-thing one sets one's mind to do. Because most Americans want to be successful, Jakes uses his personal testimony of transcending poverty to convince his listeners that they too can be blessed by God if they are faithful. He inspires his listeners to believe they are destined for greatness because God is working on their behalf to maximize their moments. Thus, Jakes uses theological princi-ples that appeal to the American mentality of success and pros-perity.

The Liberationist Critique

In the spirit of nineteenth-century abolitionist Frederick Dou-glass and nineteenth-century social thinker Karl Marx, Christians of a liberationist perspective challenge the systemic arrangements that justify the wealth of the elite and keep certain segments of a population in perpetual poverty. Like Marxists, liberationists un-cover what they perceive as the systemic misunderstanding of cap-italist society and expose the ways this misunderstanding sanctions oppression in society (West 2003). Liberationists con-tend that, like heads of multinational corporations promote capi-talist ideas that justify their own excessive wealth, prosperity preachers like Jakes promote a religious ideology that link God's favor with their wealth.

It is therefore not surprising that liberationists like James Forbes, the distinguished pastor of Riverside Church in New York City, find fault with prosperity theology. Forbes commented:

> It is clear to me that where you preach a prosperity gospel you may not be as keen to ask, "Who got left out of the formula and why does poverty sustain itself? The answers given in these circles are probably not as informed by the ancient prophets as they ought to be or by a Marxist understanding of how means of production may actually capture and hold hostage people to a materialistic

dialectic rather than a more broadly understood spirituality of Acts chapter 2, verse 2. (Interview)

Jakes has not escaped the scrutiny from liberationists who believe his prosperity gospel and individualistic focus ignore the structural constraints that prevent thousands of oppressed individuals from excelling. Religion scholar Rodney Sadler criticized Jakes and other prosperity preachers for focusing less on a gospel that reaches people in the context of community and more on a gospel that is in conjunction with capitalism. Sadler added:

Jakes' theology is very much capitalist driven. This notion of a man flying around the country in private planes and preaching a gospel that is very much tied to prosperity as opposed to preaching a gospel that's more akin to liberation of people from suffering communities, somewhat troubles me. (Interview)

James Cone, the chief architect of black liberation theology, explained how Jakes' conservative message avoids challenging the interests of those in power:

T.D. Jakes represents a black man who has strong crossover appeal but he also represents blacks who preach a gospel that is hardly distinguished from the whites and that would make it very difficult for him to have an understanding of the gospel that would be conflictive and engaging politically in a sharp sense that would cause people to be challenged in a way that makes them feel uncomfortable. (Interview)

Like Cone and Forbes, religion scholar and pastor Brad Braxton alluded to the missing justice component in Jakes' preaching:

In the messages I've heard, the focus tends to be on the individual, and I have not heard many of his messages that are addressing some of the systemic issues. To be sure, his sermons go into the prison, like when he does Woman Thou Art Loosed. How can it not touch a Christian's heart when you see women of all races and ages who are incarcerated sitting in the correctional institution around the television being blessed and excited about hearing preaching and the gospel? That's rich and I'm not going to knock that, but I'm also going to ask when are we going to hear sermons by Jakes that call into question the whole prison culture of how corporate America is getting fat on building prisons and why African American boys are going to prison at an alarmingly faster rate than white boys? When do you hear those kind of messages? (Interview)

Similarly, in an article in *Christianity Today*, activist preacher Eugene Rivers voiced his concern that Jakes is only promoting middle-class consumerism rather than offering a developed sense of biblical justice. The same article included evangelist John Perkins' warning that Jakes' prosperity teachings can be very dangerous to African Americans.

A large part of Jakes' success resides in his ability to incorporate touchstones of American culture, but that skill also generates the criticism that he advocates an American gospel. Liberationists contend that Jakes' prosperity theology is inapplicable to Christians in poverty-stricken countries like Guatemala and Nicaragua who may have abundant faith but few opportunities for social mobility. Similarly, they perceive Jakes' emphasis on human agency and self-determination as incompatible with social conditions in Bosnia, Nicaragua, Tanzania, and in many other geopolitical contexts requiring a dramatic restructuring of society for individual agency to be relevant. With this line of reasoning, liberationists assert that if you are a farmer in Afghanistan or East Africa, you will probably be a farmer for the rest of your life, and if you are one of the millions of wretchedly poor and uneducated people in South East Asia, opportunities for self-actualization and attaining greatness are dramatically limited no matter how much faith you have.

To put it more simply, liberationists contend that if Jakes' prosperity gospel were universally true, it would be equally applicable to all Christians irrespective of their class, education, and social context. God's desire to bless believers with wealth would work the same in Tanzania as it would in the United States. But rather than promoting a universal theology that applies to all people in all milieus, liberationists claim that Jakes offers a provincial gospel that works best in countries like the United States where people have the ability to acquire wealth. Even in such free-market societies, social stratification hinders masses of people from transcending their socioeconomic status.

In this fashion, T.A. Body playfully reminds his congregation that "the prosperity gospel doesn't work in the ghetto," suggesting that great faith will not overcome the structural constraints that keep masses of inner-city people impoverished. Liberationists contend that Jakes and other prosperity preachers are offering "fools' gold" by linking faith to financial success because many faithful Christians will always lack the ability to transcend structural constraints on their economic plight. Other critics believe the prosperity gospel transforms Christ's teachings into the ideals of consumer culture.

Liberationists believe that preachers like Jakes have a somewhat unsophisticated understanding of world markets and often overlook how one society's prosperity may be on the backs of poor people on the other side of the globe. The following excerpt from his sermon series "You Don't Have to Believe in my Dream" reveals Jakes' myopic approach to African poverty that omits how the exploitive powers of capitalism and colonialism contributed to Africans' inability to profit from their natural resources:

Many of you remind me of Africa, the richest continent in this world. Full of the greatest minerals, gold, diamonds, the greatest resources in the world are in Africa, not Europe, not America, in Africa. The greatest wealth in the earth is not where the highest skyscrapers are, where the most technology is, where the most aircrafts are, it is not over here, it is over there, and yet they are in almost total poverty because they have not learned how to mine what they have on the inside of them and until you learn how to pull out of you what God put in you, you will live like a pauper and people with less will do more until you know how to get it out. You sitting up there starving to death, you got diamonds, you got gold; people are using you to build their kingdom. People are walking in and out of your life taking your stuff. . . . The whole economy of the continent of Africa would be completely corrected if you could remove corruption and also draw from the resources that are intrinsically in the continent.

With this kind of preaching, Jakes promotes bourgeois thinking that overlooks how Western imperialism and exploitation contributed to Third World poverty. Similarly, Jakes' focus on individual agency fails to consider how Western prosperity and materialism are interconnected with sweatshops in Malaysia and slave labor throughout Indonesia.

Like many prosperity preachers, rather than addressing the systemic structural problems that produce poverty, Jakes often conveys poverty as the product of demonic oppression:

> I broke the spirit of poverty over my house by giving my tithes and giving my offerings. I beat the devil out of my checkbook and pleaded the blood over my finances. I scraped and crawled my way up out of poverty and into God's prosperity by doing what God said to do! And you can too. (Jakes 1997a:148)

Rather than treating poverty as a residual component of a capitalist society, Jakes depicts poverty as a spiritual ailment that can be overcome with prayer, faithful giving, and positive confession. His individualism also overlooks the structural forces behind such inner-city ills as unemployment:

> I see absolutely no excuse today for a man not to have a job. If there isn't a job available in your community that's suited to your educational level, find a job that's lower than your educational level and fill it until a better one opens up. If it's not illegal, and it's not sin, go for it. (Jakes 1997a:157)

Some may suggest Jakes' conservatism is a dose of tough love necessary for poverty-stricken individuals to pursue the American dream. But liberationists call for a more sophisticated analysis of unemployment to uncover how corporate greed, automation, and the overseas flight of manufacturing jobs contribute to joblessness in inner cities all over America.

Supporters of Jakes, however, contend that his national prison ministry, plans for a rehabilitation and jobs complex in South Dallas, plus his economic empowerment seminars nationwide demonstrate a new kind of liberationist agenda that can address the challenges people face in the twenty-first century. Such supporters contend that Jakes' approach is appropriate for contemporary African Americans who are now more preoccupied with protected growth investments than protest marches for voting rights. Jakes' former staff member, David Yeazell, hailed him as the new voice for African Americans:

> Just from observation you've got your Jesse Jackson and others who are from another generation, and the message that they proclaim is a message from another generation, and this generation is listening more to someone like Bishop Jakes because he's much more where people are at, and the last generation's civil rights message does not resonate with this generation in the same way that it used to; the issues are different. (Interview)

Likewise, biblical scholar Renita Weems presented a hypothetical counterargument against liberationists who criticize Jakes for not having a social justice component to his ministry:

Maybe he has gone over in another extreme to talk about agency with his "just pull yourself up from your bootstraps" message. Maybe perhaps he has gone further than I would want on that because I am enough of a product of the sixties and seventies to understand questions about social justice and speaking to the powers that be. But I suspect someone like him might make the argument, "but on the other hand, those of you who are mainline and traditional and who are the spokesmen for the black church, you also have made black people think of themselves as victimized so much that there was nothing that they could do except wait on God and white people to deliver them." (Interview)

Religion scholar Leonard Lovett added that Jakes' message is profoundly social and reflects a new form of black liberation by teaching African Americans creative ways to self-actualize. To counter liberationists' belief that Jakes' prosperity gospel controverts the underpinnings of prophetic ministry, New Jersey pastor Donald Hilliard made the case that Jakes offers an alternative model of liberation that complements the black church's prophetic model of attacking oppressive systems:

I would just say that every one of us doesn't have the same mantle. I think that his mantle is to do what he is doing, to raise people up individually and then they can speak to power structures. Some of our focus is on the individual piece. James Forbes focuses more so on dealing with those structural systems that oppress. Jakes deals with more of the personal things that hold people down. I don't think that everyone has the same mantle, and when we start moving out of the anointing God has put on us, we really become ineffective. (Interview)

Hilliard and Lovett contended that Jakes should be credited for inspiring African Americans to be tenacious and relentless toward achieving success. Jakes' prosperity gospel and emphasis on personal agency resonate with millions of Americans born and raised in the midst of free-market economics.

Similar to how sociologists debate whether culture or social structure plays a stronger role in determining life choices, Christians quarrel over the biblical approach to alleviating social inequality, oppression, and poverty. Those of a liberationist perspective find Jakes' connection between Christianity and capitalism to be problematic and claim that his social agenda is not based on a systemic analysis of social inequality. Counterarguments suggest Jakes preaches a new kind of liberationist message that is somewhat relevant to contemporary struggles in competitive capitalistic environs. This discussion could spark a fruitful interchange between Jakes and a liberationist like James Forbes about strategic ways to blend a much-needed emphasis on individual agency with sophisticated systems analysis, a dialogue in which Forbes has already expressed great interest:

> I would say that if I were in conversation with T.D. Jakes for a long time, I would probably engage in some effort to see whether or not he has much energy for systems analysis, and if he does that would be an interesting conversation. That is, to what extent is the gospel that he preaches actually calling people to strive to get out of poverty, and to what extent does he understand what sustains the poverty system and who benefits from it? I respect him enough to believe that I could have a very good qualitative exchange and I'm sure I'd learn something in the process. He may pick up perhaps a little deeper systems analysis from the conversation. (Interview)

Fred Price and the profusion of word churches brought changes among neo-Pentecostals that prepared the way for Jakes' message and ministry as a prosperity preacher and entrepreneur. The prosperity gospel encouraged many African Americans to view their increasing success and wealth as constituents of their Christian faith. This created an atmosphere encouraging many pastors, church leaders, and congregants to engage in a "name it and claim it" or "confess it and possess it" materialistic religious culture. This also gave the new contingency of middle- and upper-class African Americans a religious home among neo-Pentecostals rather than with Episcopalians or other groups associated with black elites in past generations.

The prosperity gospel has a particular resonance in our culture of materialism. Black prosperity preachers continue to live like CEOs of Fortune 500 companies while encouraging their members to confess and possess the same financial prosperity. But as we learned, prosperity preaching has vehement detractors. In 1996, Jakes' materialism was manifested by his purchase of fancy cars and a mansion with an indoor bowling alley and swimming pool and sparked a series of editorials in local newspapers that played a crucial role in driving him out of West Virginia. Pastors nationwide are critical of prosperity teachings, arguing that God is not a genie at our command, but a sovereign ruler who makes demands and requires sacrifices. Christians of a liberationist perspective argue that socioeconomic status is less an issue of faith and more an indication of the structural arrangements that reproduce an unequal distribution of wealth and resources. Although pastors differ in the degree to which they embrace capitalistic ideals, the prosperity message has become a force in neo-Pentecostal churches nationwide.

Jakes offers an American gospel that supports the status quo and sits well with bourgeois democratic American sensibilities. *Time* magazine's comparison of Jakes to Billy Graham is telling because liberationists like Cone and Forbes have also criticized Graham for preaching an American gospel of personal salvation and for failing to challenge segregation and the Vietnam War. Like Graham and many conservative preachers, Jakes makes liberation the individual's responsibility rather than offering a sophisticated systems analysis of poverty and oppression. This should not be surprising in light of Jakes' penchant for peppering his message with touchstones of the American experience. The

American motifs of self-determination and individualism were important in Jakes' personal struggle out of poverty, therefore it is not astonishing that such themes reverberate throughout his message and ministry. One might also add that it is not in Jakes' best interests as a multimillionaire to challenge the status quo, and, hence, protecting his financial empire calls for preaching a conservative message.

[6]

"Woman Art Thou Really Loosed?"

After attending one of his conferences, the operative question
comes to mind, "Woman art thou really loosed?"
                                                    —Anonymous pastor

Included in the press packet journalists received at one of Jakes'
recent conferences is the claim that Woman Thou Art Loosed 99
was the largest gathering of Christian women in world history.
Though this claim is difficult to verify, the fact that Jakes draws
tens of thousands of followers from cities nationwide to yearly
conferences for women demonstrates his tremendous influence.
Candy Wilson, a three-time attendee, believes Jakes' vast appeal
centers on his ability to articulate a message to women in pain:

> Women all over have never been able to express why they are
> the way they are; why they hurt, why they go through the same
> cycle over and over, and Bishop touches the hearts of where
> women are emotionally and spiritually. I believe that is part of
> the reason he has such an appeal to people, especially women.
> (Interview)

Jakes' childhood experiences made him sensitive to many of the
women's issues he addresses each year via his conferences, books,
videos, songs, and sermons. Though Jakes was not the product of
a single-parent family, his father spent most of his waking hours
working, and therefore his mother Odith practically raised her

children alone. By spending so much time with his mother, Jakes learned firsthand the difficulties of a woman running a household while enduring a deteriorating marriage. Jakes' ministry as shepherd to the shattered began with consoling his mother through the trying days of taking care of an invalid husband and through the difficult period after the divorce.

In both his storefront church in Montgomery and after moving to Smithers, Jakes preached to many lonely women abandoned by husbands due to drugs, alcohol, or relocation for better employment. By traversing the revival circuit of West Virginia coal-mining towns and preaching to his own church, Jakes developed an early sensitivity to struggles many women face. After detecting common threads in the stories of many women in their counseling sessions, Jakes concluded that a group therapy session in the form of a Sunday School lesson would be beneficial. In 1992 he started one called "Woman Thou Art Loosed." The lesson became a hit, with over a hundred women attending Sunday School. He began to address rape, incest, and other sensitive issues women faced, and the word spread throughout the surrounding area about the Sunday School lesson.

Jakes has always blended spirituality with personal ambition. Thus more than likely the motives for Sunday School lessons were both spiritual and strategic. He was addressing people's needs while also carving out new space for his ministry, thus blending his compassion for people in pain with his drive toward expanding his market share. Jakes would soon learn that his capacity for soothing women's pains and troubles could yield considerable dividends. By the time he received his big break on national television in the fall of 2002 and spring of 2003, he was already adept at addressing many complicated problems women faced. Hence, he would quickly corner a market that would translate into a worldwide ministry and millions in revenue.

At the time that Jakes rose to national prominence, not many prominent preachers were carefully calibrating their messages to the gender that dominated church attendance. Jakes' career exploded after he preached his now legendary sermon "Woman Thou Art Loosed" in 1993 at the AZUSA Conference. He strategically followed up on his preaching success to women by writing a book with the same title that eventually sold over a million copies and opened the door for scores of other books and videos marketed toward women.

Currently no religious figure in America can draw more women to his conferences than Jakes. With his ability to draw tens of thousands of them to his side and generate best-selling books with messages for them, it is surprising that more feminists have not scrutinized his message and ministry. One explanation derives from the fact that academics have been slow to respond to the Jakes phenomenon in general. While other preachers and journalists analyze Jakes' teachings, the academic community is apathetic about his amazing rise and widespread influence. Rather than deconstructing his message for women, many feminist theologians consider Jakes unworthy of their attention, while some are even oblivious to his mass appeal. This situation reflects the unfortunate reality that when it comes to major developments in pop culture, academics are usually the last to know.

But there is a more cogent explanation for why few feminist scholars analyze or critique Jakes' teachings. If a person suffers a gunshot wound, you do not nurse his cancerous tumor because the demands of the moment suggest you tend the wound. Likewise, many of the leading feminist theologians who are familiar with Jakes' message and ministry have deeper wounds to mend. The fact that Jakes endorses women preachers and invites them to keynote his conferences makes him far more progressive than most Baptists and Methodists, who still engage in fierce debates over whether or not God calls women to the ministry. Because of the sexism in American Protestantism, feminist theologians like Delores Williams, Jacquelyn Grant, and Kelly Brown Douglas have bigger fish to fry and thus do not exert time and energy toward forging a critical analysis of Jakes' message to women. While feminists fight for fundamental issues of equality in the church, the subtly sexist overtones of Jakes' teachings and ministry receive little analysis.

Jakes the Feminist

There is a political dimension to biblical interpretation concerning how pastors use scripture to emphasize some ideas and deemphasize others. When one weighs in on what the Bible says and considers the potential effects of particular interpretations, one can alter the balance of power in communities. The most ready-made example of the political nature of biblical hermeneutics involves the fact that slave masters and abolitionists used the same Bible to justify their positions. Similarly, women have been both embraced in spiritual leadership and denied access to the pulpit depending on how religious elites interpret scripture concerning women in ministry and how much authority they give to those passages. In light of women's ongoing political struggle for spiritual leadership, an analysis of Jakes' message to women should begin by acknowledging that in many ways he is a feminist who has given unapologetic support to women pastors.

In its most basic definition, a feminist is one who advances the cause of women's equality and fights against social systems that oppress them. Jakes' feminist inclination traces back to his childhood through the legacy of strong women in his family. Young Tommy was inspired by the example of his grandmother, who put herself through college by doing laundry. As an entrepreneur, teacher, and public speaker, Jakes' mother inspired a keen respect and appreciation for the talents and leadership capabilities of women. Jakes credits no one as much as Odith for influencing his career, as indicated by his tribute to her memory in his book *God's Leading Lady*:

There are few times when I stand to do anything in public that I cannot catch a glimpse of my mother's legacy affecting and influ-

encing my every move. At every speaking engagement, her teaching style directs my words. For every decision I am called to make,
her wisdom guides me. (Jakes 2002:228)

It is not surprising that Odith Jakes' legacy as a strong woman
and leader would inculcate feminist leanings in her son.

Initially, Jakes' childhood experience at First Baptist Church of
Vandalia did not expose him to female pastors, evangelists, or
preachers. First Baptist's longtime pastor, Paul J. Gilmore, did
not allow women to function as clergy. The few women who
would periodically address the congregation called themselves
missionaries rather than preachers. But when Jakes joined Greater
Emanuel Gospel Tabernacle as a teenager, he saw women in spiritual leadership and learned to take it for granted that God's calling was gender neutral. Evangelist Christine McCaskill was one
of many women who strongly influenced Jakes in his early
preaching ministry. Years later, the popular California preacher
Ernestine Reems was another woman who played a major role in
Jakes' life and ministry. The effect that McCaskill and Reems had
on Jakes also contributed to his current support for women
preachers.

Jakes gives unrelenting support for female preachers and makes
feminist statements in books and sermons:

> The glory days of yesteryear were filled with gender bias and injus-
> tice. Unfortunately, the good ole boys' club is still up and running.
> [A woman] suffered immeasurable bias and mistreatment, and in
> response she had to become a fighter. (Jakes 1998:54)

In his keynote address at Woman Thou Art Loosed 2001, Jakes
contended that the increase of women in spiritual leadership symbolizes an infusion of God's power in the church:

> When you see women rising up in the church it is a sign that we
> have come into the last days. The breaking loose of the woman is a

prophetic dimension of the glory of God, that you are going to release a glory on the body that is powerful.

His book *God's Leading Lady* is a call for women to take center
stage. It reads like a feminist treatise against the patriarchy in
American Protestantism:

> Too often women have been conditioned not to ask for what is
> rightfully theirs. Like greedy bullies on the playground, men have
> divvied up the goods among themselves, afraid of sharing their au-
> thority and riches with the female coheirs in their lives. (Jakes
> 2002:39)

In this book, Jakes argued that God is no respecter of gender, and
he offers a strong defense for God calling women to the ministry.
Jakes also discussed how women have been the driving force of
the church, and he chided men for creating a double standard in
which women "can virtually do anything that needs doing as long
as they let men have the voice and take credit for it" (Jakes
2002:41).

Jakes also included alternative interpretations of two New Testament passages that are frequently cited as biblical injunctions
against female preachers. Responding to the Apostle Paul's call
for women to remain silent in the church (1 Corinthians
14:34–35), Jakes contested that if Paul's words are to be taken
literally, then women in the church should be silenced everywhere
or nowhere at all. Jakes also addressed Paul's first letter to Timo-
thy, which precludes women from having authority over men and
admonishes women to learn in quietness and full submission (1
Tim 2:8–15). Jakes argued that Paul's principles are timeless, but
his examples are local and encouraged women to continue exer-
cising their ministry gifts under God's unction. Jakes added that
there is a new breed of men coming who will support women in
spiritual leadership, and he exhorted women not to remain silent
in the church.

Jakes challenges women to dream big, act toward their own interests, be more assertive, and enjoy more personal agency. In his keynote address at the New Orleans Essence Festival in 2002, Jakes urged each woman to "take yourself out to dinner, encourage yourself, love yourself, treat yourself right," and to be a victor, not a victim. Jakes persuades women to believe that they are significant, that their needs and dreams matter, and that they should not wait around for Prince Charming to sweep them off their feet. Jakes also created intelligent and ambitious female characters in his first novel, *Cover Girls,* and gives valuable tips to women preachers in his God's Leading Lady tours in cities nationwide.

Jakes' church in Dallas has had talented women on staff. Rita Twiggs is an assistant pastor and Charlene Burgess an Old Testament professor. It is not uncommon for women like Joyce Meyer, Paula White, Claudette Copeland, and Suzie Owens to preach at his conferences. Because the church has perpetuated male hegemony in spiritual leadership, a moderate feminist like Jakes appears to be quite radical in his attack on patriarchy. But like most postmodern thinkers, Jakes often holds contrasting perspectives in tension. One such complexity involves the fact that although Jakes has done much to fight for gender equality, his prescriptions for women often perpetuate sexism.

Jakes the Antifeminist

Whereas the term "sex" refers to the biological differences between men and women, "gender" alludes to the norms, values, and social positions that a society prescribes for being a male or a female. One does not have to be a social scientist to recognize that most societies are structured along gender lines. The cultural anthropologist Margaret Mead's studies on different tribes in New Guinea did much to confirm that gender is organized through social interaction and therefore differs from society to society. Mead's constructionist approach repudiated the idea that gender differences have natural origins and suggested there is no objective way to be male or female because culture influences the way people perceive gender. Conversely, a person who maintains an essentialist approach to gender assumes that gender norms are derived through nature or God. In other words, gender essentialists believe there is an essence to being male and female that does not vary from society to society but that defines the very nature, purpose, and function of each gender.

Historically, patriarchal (male-dominated) societies have contended that God or nature designed certain functions for each gender. For example, for much of our nation's history men were assigned the "natural" task of protecting and leading, and women were often relegated to childbearing and nurturing. Contemporary American movies and television often show women as innately emotional and less logical than men, implicitly suggesting women are less capable of leading. Although gender equality is still far off, feminist movements of the nineteenth and twentieth centuries did much to challenge essentialist prescriptions for women that limited their opportunities for self-actualization and leadership.

Though Jakes supports female pastors and leaders and encourages women to be master of their own fates, his teachings often endorse gender essentialism. Like John Gray's popular book *Men Are from Mars, Women Are from Venus* became a cultural phenomenon by elevating gender differences, Jakes promotes the essentialist idea that God created women with different purposes and functions than men. Jakes draws a great deal of his conclusions about gender differences from events that took place in the biblical account of the Garden of Eden:

> One of the great differences between men and women is rooted in this: Man had position with God before he had a relationship with another human being. Woman was birthed in a relationship. We see today that men are positional and women are relational. (Jakes 1997a:45)

Jakes continued to discuss how men are far more preoccupied with power and status and women are more concerned about relationships:

> When men get together they ask one another, "What do you do for a living?" In the course of the conversation, they expect to find out what position another man holds in his company. When women get together they ask, "Are you married? Do you have children?" (Ibid.)

Rather than viewing those alleged gender differences as residue of patriarchal socialization and women's historical exclusion from career opportunities, Jakes presents them as natural distinctions created by God in the Garden of Eden. He perpetuates the idea that men and women are profoundly different, and that God has given him special insight on women.

Much of Jakes' advice to women involves essentialist notions of masculinity and femininity. Jakes argues that though it was a mistake of the past for men to oppress women, the mistake of the future is "this spirit whereby the woman imitates the masculine strength and we lose the creative edge of her feminine perspectives" (Jakes 1998:60). Jakes portrays softness as part of the essence of a woman:

> Man was created with the woman hidden in his being. God then skillfully brings out of him that hidden part called woman. She was taken "out of him." Her removal left a void and this creates man's attraction for her. She was the softer side of him. She was his tenderness, and those emotions he couldn't share. (Jakes 1998:56)

Jakes' gender prescriptions often convey the idea that God made men to be strong and aggressive and women to be tender. In one book Jakes argued it is sin for a man to "misrepresent himself" by conducting himself as a woman:

> I am not merely speaking of homosexuality. I am also talking
> about men who are feminine in their mannerism. Many of these
> men may not be homosexual in their behavior, but the Bible says
> that they must be healed of feminine mannerisms, or vice versa. It
> is equally sad to see a masculine woman. (Jakes 1997[1993]:12)

Jakes also contends that God created women to be weaker vessels,
but not weakness in terms of substandard, but in terms of being
more "satin-like" in a manner tantamount to a silk shirt being
more delicate and more valuable than a cotton one (Jakes
1996a:35). Jakes justifies the latter distinction of women as softer
by quoting the biblical admonition for husbands to honor their
wives as weaker vessels (1 Peter 3:7).

In his best-seller *The Lady, Her Lover, and Her Lord,* Jakes
urges women to be strong but adds the caveat that the woman
has strength in silk wrappings. He longs for the gentle femininity
of the past "that once sat on porches and sipped tea in the gentle
breezes of softer times" (Jakes 1998:60). He often depicts
women as sophisticated caretakers of men and children and uses
his mother as the primary example of how to be a good home-
maker. Jakes portrays it as natural for men to be hard and aggressive while urging women to be girlish and kittenish, asserting that
a feminine man or masculine female goes against God's intended
functions for men and women.

At first glance, Jakes' depiction of women as the softer side of
men may appear harmless to most individuals conditioned in a patriarchal culture that has regarded women as nurturers and caretakers for centuries. But his notions of femininity do much to
limit women's creativity in defining their own physicality, personal style, sexuality, and life options. Are tennis champions like
Venus and Serena Williams, boxing greats like Lucia Rijker and
Laila Ali, and basketball stars like Chandi Jones and Nikki Mc-
Cray any less feminine because they are physically fit, strong, and
extremely competitive? How would Jakes counsel these female
athletes to be "feminine" and not "masculine"? Jakes fails to con-

sider that masculinity and femininity are socially defined and vary in different contexts. Pink may be considered a feminine color in the United States but masculine in other parts of the world. Equally, men may be open and free to shed tears in one country while they risk being perceived as feminine for such an open display of emotion in other countries. Hence, Jakes overlooks that what is deemed as masculine or feminine is an ongoing social construction and therefore does not necessarily have to be rooted in God's will.

Jakes' clout as a feminist is also diminished when one considers the titles of some of his best-selling books and his conferences dedicated to women. He has used "Woman Thou Art Loosed" for a movie, a book, a play, a CD, yearly conferences, T-shirts, and other paraphernalia, though such a title alludes that a man has the formula to set women free from all that binds them. One should detect the implicit difference between the passive title "Woman Thou Art Loosed" and the virulent symbolism in "Manpower!," the name of his yearly conferences for men. The fact that Jakes titled one of his books *Daddy Loves His Girls* may be equally unsettling to feminists considering the book is targeted to adult women. The following excerpt conveys how the recurring theme of *Daddy Loves His Girls* insinuates that the God of the universe will make everything better for delicate, anxious, and hurting women desiring love and protection from their earthly fathers:

> In this world of broken homes and trembling relationships, it is important that we don't lose complete definition of a father's love. His strong arms pick you up when you are low. In those arms you nestle as he carries you to bed when sleep has claimed you on the couch. (Jakes 1996a:17)

The symbolism evoked with Jakes' depiction of a divine male authority figure being the psychoemotional fulcrum for weak and feeble daddy's girls does little to promote feminist or egalitarian ideals. In this book, Jakes speaks with a paternalistic tone to address what he frames as the complex issues of womanhood.

An important component of Jakes' sexism stems from his interpretation of biblical passages that project the man as the head of his household. In his book *So You Call Yourself a Man?* Jakes uses patriarchal language to urge husbands to take spiritual authority in their homes:

> Take authority over your finances today. Rebuke the devil in the name of Jesus, give your tithes and offerings—as the man and priest of your house, and then look for God's blessing to be poured out from heaven on you. (Jakes 1997a:149)

The designation "priest" of the home denotes ultimate spiritual authority over the well-being of the family and is in conflict with an egalitarian vision of parental leadership based on consensus. Jakes argues that God will restore order in the home when men take their proper place of leadership. This type of rhetoric resembles the ideology promoted by Promise Keepers, an evangelical movement that encourages men to take back control of their families and their nation. Jakes keynoted crusades for Promise Keepers in the mid-1990s and is a proponent of their belief that God has a preeminent place for male leadership.

As one of his seven tips to help career women balance their careers and families, Jakes admonished women to honor their husbands. Jakes cited Ephesians 5:22–28 to show that wives are supposed to submit to their husbands and that male headship is for women's welfare so they can feel protected and nurtured. This demonstrates that Jakes picks and chooses when to exert a feminist interpretation of scriptural mandates on gender and when to embrace the patriarchal prescriptions for gender. Jakes the feminist is flexible and creative when it comes to passages that seemingly preclude women from preaching, but Jakes the antifeminist accepts literal interpretations of scriptures that depict women as weaker vessels and men as heads and priest of their homes.

Jakes often urges wives to indulge their husbands' insecurities and fears. In his book *The Lady, Her Lover and Her Lord*, he advises the woman to keep her lover happy by not speaking bad words but to encourage and make him feel safe enough to love back. Jakes exhorts the woman in all of her interactions to do whatever it takes not to frustrate her lover for fear of driving him away:

> When he walks through the door and is assaulted by complaints, he may be tempted to walk right back out. The roof may be leaking, the baby may have cried all day, and the rent may be due, but if that's all he has to look forward to at home, he may have second thoughts about going there. (Jakes 1998:155–156)

Jakes places much of the onus on the woman for keeping her man happy and ignores the fact that women have been indulging men's needs and insecurities for too long in our patriarchal society:

> Now I'm not saying that you shouldn't share your challenges with your man, but when he comes home at night, give him a kiss on the cheek, let him sit in a chair, and tell him how glad you are to see him. If he doesn't feel welcomed at home, he may find another place to hang his hat. This is when the "other woman" becomes so enticing. (Jakes 1998:155–156)

In the same book, Jakes contends that women are by nature communicators, homemakers, weaker, more susceptible to Satan's deceptions, and the bearer of maternal instincts that often lead them to the role of giver. In perhaps his most shocking prescription, Jakes makes a case that the wife should always let her husband be the breadwinner of the family, lest she reverse the family order and cause the family unit to go into chaos:

> Misplaced contribution tears down family order. It is not good for the man to eat out of the woman's hand. Anytime the woman is

the primary breadwinner it destroys the man's self-esteem. It does-n't matter who makes the most money as much as it matters that he assumes the chief responsibility for provision. (Jakes 1998:90)

Jakes added that a man becomes confused, guilty, and angry when he is not the chief provider for his family. To prevent such male angst from occurring, Jakes provided his solution for wives who make more money than their husbands:

Now, I'm not saying that a woman shouldn't work and earn money. In fact, you may make more money than your husband. But take that money and save it, spend it, use it to buy stocks or fancy vacations. Just don't let your husband feel as if he has not provided for his own. (Jakes 1998:90–91)

Hence, Jakes encourages women to spend their money on fancy vacations rather using the money for bills to avoid deflating their husbands' egos as breadwinners. This message once again places the onus on the woman to coddle her husband's insecurities.

Another aspect of Jakes' antifeminism involves his penchant for treating women as objects of beauty. He often paints alluring pictures to poetically expound on female beauty and often makes awkward references to women's breasts. For example, while the Bible is silent about Adam and Eve's physical dimensions, Jakes used literary license to portray an evocative picture of Eve in one of his books:

The only thing that covered her soft, satiny skin was the bright yellow rays of the sun. In the night, the moonlight cradled her breast with tender hands and a radiant glow. . . . As she ran, her strong thighs whipped through the tall grain with a synergy that cannot be adequately described. (Jakes 1998:62)

A few paragraphs later Jakes makes another reference to Eve's breasts:

[Eve] was planned and crafted to the slightest detail. [God] designed her cycles and systems. He designed her breasts and their function. (Jakes 1998:63)

Jakes refers to women's breasts four times alone in his book *Daddy Loves His Girls*, and here is one example:

My advice for you, daughter, is to be prepared for change. . . . There is no escaping it. The firm breasts that were once small lumps will inflate with child-rearing and deflate in later years. (Jakes 1996a:77)

Whether he is referring to strong thighs, firm breasts, satiny skin, sex appeal, or overall beauty in general, Jakes' unnecessary references to female physicality represent the patriarchal habit of objectifying the female body.

It is generally true that oppressors rarely make adequate liberators of the oppressed. Ernestine Reems, Iona Locke, Jackie McCullough, Paula White, Juanita Bynum, Vashti McKenzie, and various popular female preachers address female issues but, with the exception of Bynum, only enjoy a small fraction of Jakes' female market share. His dominant share in this market suggests that he benefits from a patriarchal religious structure that socializes women to prefer sitting at the feet of a man to receive their spiritual breakthrough. This fact brought Delores Carpenter some chagrin in a moment of reflection at one of Jakes' earlier conferences for women:

A man championing women is a great thing for the point of advocacy, and I thought his appeal was phenomenal, but I did feel a little sad because I knew in my heart all the women who could preach the same thing but would not get that kind of response. For some reason, hearing it from a man made it more profound for the women and that made me a little sad. (Interview)

Though most feminists have been reticent concerning Jakes' message and ministry to women, some voiced strong opinions and reservations. Renita Weems, a noted feminist biblical scholar, provided a humorous yet penetrating description of how Jakes' message differs from that of women preachers:

> But the truth is that when you listen to the women preaching, even the most Pentecostal of the women, they are not preaching the same thing that Jakes preaches. The women preachers go a little bit further and tell women, "Go back home and turn that house out." "Put the rascal out." Jakes never questions patriarchy and he never tells you to go put a Negro out. Now, he would tell you go back, get yourself together, believe God, walk in there with pride, all that, but the sisters will say, "You tell that nigger if he puts his hand on you again, whatever you've got to do just do it!" That's the difference; Jakes is not messing up any man's house! He stops short. (Interview)

Similarly, Delores Williams, one of the chief architects of what has been coined womanist theology, a feminist camp of theology targeted to the unique struggles of black women, offered a critique of Jakes' message and ministry to women:

> Jakes' approach to women reinforces the same old stereotypes of women's roles, but only saying that, women, "You don't have to take abuse in any of these roles." At least what I've seen and read of his work it doesn't get beyond the role of woman being woman as she always has been defined. But there is also a subtext to his work, which I think is a resounding innuendo more than a straightforward developed idea and that is, "Women you are freed for choice, but choice within this particular range of options." Women's consciousness has not been sufficiently raised to be able to see these subtleties that claim that you're free when you're not free. So much of the theology in our churches is still tied up in biblical prescriptions for what a woman ought to be and how a

woman ought to behave that have nothing to do with social reality today but everything to do with social reality in the time of Paul. (Interview)

Williams believes that Jakes' ministry and message make women emotionally dependent upon him; an opinion also offered by a popular pastor in the Midwest:

> I've got a lot of members in my church that will go to Jake's conference every year. They will spend hundreds, thousands of dollars on bus tickets, plane tickets, four or five nights in a hotel, buying all of his books for him to tell them that they are loosed and they come back four and five thousand dollars more in debt than they were before, and that's when they come to my church asking me for rent. (Interview)

This is an important criticism because it alludes to Jakes as the surrogate "man." For countless women he may be the only man to say positive things and to encourage them.

Critical analysis of Jakes' message to women is long overdue when considering his remarkable appeal. On the one hand, we should contextualize Jakes within the overarching religious patriarchy and present him on the vanguard of feminism among Protestant preachers. Jakes speaks out on certain issues regarding women and even makes a place for female preachers. But at the same time we should also note the sexist overtones and patriarchal ideas in Jakes' message that controvert feminist ideals. Reinforcing essentialist notions of gender, romanticizing a bygone era of female femininity, and reflecting on women as weaker vessels can obstruct feminist goals of transcending traditional gender norms that were established predominantly by men. Jakes offers a conflicting message to women that empowers and impairs, humanizes and objectifies, one that often looses and yet sometimes binds.

[7]

Businessman and a Minister

I began the interview by attempting to explain that I have preached the gospel like Paul from all economic levels. I have been abased and abounded. . . . I attempted to explain that I am both a businessman and a minister. God has bountifully blessed both of these areas.   —T.D. Jakes

The Jakes phenomenon began when he was a young child peddling vegetables from his mother's garden years before he turned spirituality into a multimillion dollar industry. As his former neighbor Bobbie Tolliver observed, "Tommy has been selling something ever since he was six or seven years old, and he was very good at it." Though Jakes' emergence is the fortuitous blending of time and opportunity, his organizational savvy and strategic marketing helped him become one of the most prolific spiritual leaders in the country. But maintaining his entrepreneurial machine creates pressure to generate the resources for large staffs and creative marketing initiatives. This often compels Jakes the businessman to make crafty decisions to protect and expand his market share.

Jakes' amazing ascent came during a time when spiritual leaders operate multidimensional ministries like major corporations and utilize mass media and commercial networks to produce spiritual commodities for mass consumption. Today, Christians are inundated with spiritual images in the same way that Americans are passive victims of television advertisements for Viagra, push-up bras, and flashy sports cars. Celebrity preachers like John Hagee and Joel Osteen run large ministries that generate millions every month, and pastors of mega churches use elaborate mailing lists and expensive full-page ads in *Charisma* magazine to market their conferences and meetings to millions of Christians each year. These preachers promote their ministries on TBN and Daystar, the two largest Christian TV networks. As a result, they enjoy million-dollar lifestyles. No other minister characterizes our post-modern age of commercialized spirituality more than T.D. Jakes.

Americans have been ambivalent about Jakes' flamboyant brand of Christianity. While many support him, critics contend he has gone too far in bridging the secular and the sacred. While many embrace his message of prosperity, some argue that Jakes' enormous popularity and worldly success prove that he offers a trendy message with no prophetic edge. While supporters believe he represents an innovative style of Christianity that speaks to contemporary Americans, detractors assert that by endorsing consumerism and carnal pleasures, Jakes breeds enmity against God. Jakes' penchant for polarizing Christians characterizes the theme of this book—that he generates both popularity and criticism for being profoundly American.

Jakes is part of a faith industry producing spiritual commodities that resonate with the American masses. Since his rise from obscurity in 1992, Jakes has been almost unerring in addressing the needs and tastes of his listeners and accordingly has reaped great financial rewards. Thousands nationwide have craved his books, videos, and tapes. Almost everything bearing Jakes' name has sold like hotcakes. Jakes built an entrepreneurial machine by commercializing spirituality and thus has demonstrated more than any contemporary religious figure that religion is marketable and profitable.

Jakes expresses no moral qualms about living a life of luxury off the proceeds from religious followers. Although many of his followers overlook the commercial aspect of his identity and mission,

Jakes has never been shy about his role as a businessman. His early conferences demonstrated a surprising blend of spirituality and capitalism, as discussed by Lisa Evans who attended one at the Charleston Civic Center in 1995:

> But what impressed me when I went down to West Virginia was that before you could get into the auditorium, there were all of these T-shirts, tapes, books—it's this big commercial kind of marketplace scene before you could even get into the services. I was very struck by that. I had never seen a black preacher have that kind of merchandising going along with a conference. (Interview)

If you attend any of Jakes' conferences or visit the Potter's House on Sunday morning, you will see a myriad of people after the service peddling Jakes' wares in the lobby and bookstore.

Jakes often justifies his million-dollar lifestyle with the fact that much of his wealth comes from his businesses rather than from his salary as pastor of the Potter's House, thereby drawing a line between business and ministry:

> I am very blessed. I have my ministry, which is my passion, and I have business success, which is the result of my creativity and the source of my financial success. For years I have worked beyond my church with businesses and companies exploring creativity without forsaking my calling to the ministry. (Jakes 2000:41)

Jakes reiterated his role as a businessman during a television interview on CNN:

> I own three companies. I've got a production company. And entrepreneurial pursuits are very, very important to me, to my culture, to my family, to my community, and yet I'm still a preacher. And to me, success is being able to do everything that's inside of you, and not just to be stereotypically bound to one aspect or one

talent of your life. Everybody has more than one talent, and they
need to dig it out. (CNN, *Live at Daybreak*, September 10, 2001)

Jakes' talent includes commodifying his ministry and convincing
his customers to perceive him as a man of God. In other words,
Jakes' businesses and ministry both depend on his followers believing that his words are from God.

Jakes offers a postmodern association of religion and capitalism
by craftily marketing Christianity with techniques one might learn
at Kellogg Business School. Jakes the minister preaches powerful
sermons that soothe hurting souls while Jakes the businessman
writes books, burns CDs, sells videos, and garners generous honorariums to amass a personal fortune. But there may be intrinsic
challenges involved with such a marriage between business and
ministry. A businessperson knows there are only a limited number
of consumers, so he or she strives to corner as much of the market
as possible through innovation and strategic promotion. Aggressive efforts to expand market share become more complicated
when one is in the business of saving souls and touching hearts. It
is to Jakes' benefit to keep people attracted to his products because he is competing with other "businesspersons" for market
share. Thus the convergence of Jakes the businessman with Jakes
the preacher necessitates strategic marketing to sell the gospel and
keep the empire solvent.

Such spiritual machines are forced to perpetuate large amounts
of money to support their elaborate infrastructures. This reality
has the potential to compel spiritual leaders to make decisions
generated by financial necessity to keep their machines well oiled
and functioning. For example, almost twenty years ago, the pressure of maintaining his $250 million empire led Oral Roberts to
declare prophetically that he would face imminent death if he did
not raise millions of dollars by a certain date. Similarly, after a pu-
rification process in prison, Jim Bakker discussed at AZUSA 95
how the demands of sustaining his million-dollar television ministry contributed to his financial impropriety. Likewise, Jakes has

not escaped the pressures of making financial decisions to protect and expand his spiritual machine.

An early example of Jakes' business-like mindset spawned negative publicity in a West Virginia newspaper. On April 12, 1995, the *Charleston Gazette* ran an article by Lawrence Messina with the headline, "Televangelist Tries to Evict Couple from Home." The article discussed how Jakes and his brother purchased a property at an Internal Revenue Service auction in November 1994, after which the previous owners had only one week to pay off the tax debt in order to keep their house. The article portrayed the Jakes brothers as business moguls ordering the previous owners to vacate the premises with no place to go so they could profit from renting the property to other people. The Jakes brothers' response was printed in the article:

> We're within the rules and regulations. We're not out of line. It's just normal business, just business. We buy and sell real estate all the time. It's not anybody taking advantage of anybody.

The article closed with a plea to Jakes from the previous owner: "If he's such a good person, why is he picking on us? We just want to stay in our house." The Jakes brothers ignored their plea and put business before charity. Other salient examples have shown Jakes applying a business-first mentality to protect or expand his market share.

Jakes and Carlton Pearson

Most national ministries thrive through the largesse of their donor bases. Donor lists are the lifeline of television ministries and therefore are protected as sacred property. Jakes' ambitious quest to expand his market share in 1994 led him to use another ministry's donor list, an action that is taboo in televangelism. Carlton Pearson had established an expansive mailing list of supporters that helped offset the cost of his TBN program and other ministry expenses. In 1994, a disgruntled associate quit working for Pearson's ministry (the AZUSA Fellowship) but not before sabotaging video tapes and misappropriating the entire mailing list. This former associate began working for T.D. Jakes shortly after breaking with AZUSA, according to Pearson and another former associate. Before long, Pearson received word that Jakes was using the stolen mailing list in his fund-raising efforts.

When Pearson confronted Jakes about the mailing list, Jakes was repentant, claiming he had not known that his new mailing list was procured unethically. Pearson exonerated him of premeditated misconduct and conveyed to me that Jakes' humble apology rectified the situation. But in light of the organizational and marketing savvy that Jakes demonstrated in the early 1990s to build his empire, it is difficult to imagine him innocently accepting a mailing list from a former AZUSA associate without inquiring of its origins. Jakes' unrelenting quest to expand his market share by raising enough money to stay on national television was enough incentive, at the very least, to prevent him from asking too many questions about the source of his new mailing list.

Another example of market share over ministry involves Jakes' more recent detachment from Carlton Pearson. The fact that Jakes has not been as forthright publicly about Pearson's critical role in launching his career is troubling considering Jakes' good fortune that resulted from their association. Whether on his Web page or in interviews for articles in the *Washington Post*, *Wall Street Journal*, *Time*, or *Christianity Today*, Jakes describes his rise to prominence as a gradual progression from conducting Sunday School lessons to writing the best-selling book, *Woman Thou Art Loosed*. He always omits the concurrent events involving Pearson's influence that made his rise to fame possible. In the first chapter of *God's Leading Lady*, Jakes makes one of only a few public references to his big break at AZUSA 93, but does so without mentioning Pearson's name.

Months after our interview, I contacted Pearson to discuss this oversight in Jakes' book. Pearson was surprised and disappointed and guessed that Jakes was trying to distance himself from Pearson's recent doctrinal controversy. Pearson has become a notorious figure in neo-Pentecostal circles of late and Jakes undoubtedly chose to exclude his name to protect his market share. This choice of self-advancement over acknowledging the man most responsible for his amazing rise reflects the recurring tension between Jakes the anointed man of God and Jakes the shrewd and calculated businessman who protects his financial portfolio at all cost.

Jakes and Doctrinal Criticism

Another example of Jakes' business-first approach involves his crafty response to criticism of his doctrinal stance on the Trinity. When Jakes became a member of Greater Emanuel Gospel Tabernacle as a teenager, he began a lifelong association with Apostolic movements. As we have learned, Apostolic Pentecostals reject Trinitarian doctrine, which depicts God as three persons: Father, Son, and Holy Spirit. They strongly affirm the Oneness doctrine, which portrays God as only one person, Jesus Christ. Jakes became a regional bishop for Greater Emanuel International Fellowship early in his preaching career, and later was affiliated with another anti-Trinitarian fellowship called Higher Ground Always Abounding Assemblies, which he currently serves as vice-bishop. It is inconceivable that two anti-Trinitarian associations would ordain Jakes as a bishop if he rejected the Oneness doctrine, their most distinctive tenant.

The year 2000 opened up with a *Christian Research Journal* article that was critical about Jakes and his ministry. The author, Jerry Buckner, a pastor and radio host, reproved Jakes for rejecting Trinitarian views of God. Buckner's article generated a wave of commentary in Christian magazines and journals questioning Jakes' ties to an avowed anti-Trinitarian association of churches.

Many Protestants believe Oneness doctrine is heretical, so Buckner's claim had the potential to damage Jakes' status as a reputable mainstream Christian leader. Buckner and other critics calculated that Jakes' leadership and thirty-year association with Apostolic networks suggest that he more than likely rejects the Trinity.

Rather than admitting anti-Trinitarian leanings, Jakes quickly responded to Buckner's criticism by providing a vague statement on his Web page and in a February article in *Christianity Today* on his stance on the Trinity. Jakes refused to make a definitive public statement on whether he accepts or rejects the Trinity. This ambiguity helped him weather the storm of doctrinal criticism and keep a foot in both camps. Jakes is well aware of the damage that doctrinal controversy had on Carlton Pearson's ministry and has too much business savvy to allow that to happen to him. The same way that Michael Jordan eschews political statements because he understands that both Republicans and Democrats buy Nike products, Jakes intentionally avoids being up-front about his rejection of the Trinity because that would alienate many of his followers.

Books and Videos

Jakes is part of a faith industry that packages and markets spirituality in the form of salable commodities for mass consumption. At first glance, one might be impressed with Jakes' literary accomplishment, generating so many books in a little more than ten years. But Jakes has not been forthright about the degree to which his books convey original thoughts and how much derives from other "cogs" in the Jakes machine. Like Billy Graham, Pat Robertson, and many celebrity preachers before him, Jakes often employs talented researchers and ghostwriters to help produce his books. For example, Leonard Lovett, a noted Pentecostal intellectual, not only recruited Jakes to write for a publisher of Christian books, but also ghostwrote one of Jakes' books. According to Lovett:

I ghostwrote the third book, *Water in the Wilderness*. It took me about a week sitting up in my apartment there to really write the thing and another guy took it, went over my stuff, and we passed it on to the head of Pneuma, and Jakes consented. That's how we ended up doing two or three of his other books.

Jakes later became savvier by forcing ghostwriters and assistants to sign waivers prohibiting them from discussing their contributions to his books. Accordingly, David Yeazell refused to discuss with me his contributions to one of Jakes' more recent books in fear of violating the waiver he signed. Such a waiver only serves to prevent staff contributors from going public with the full extent of their contributions to Jakes' books.

By the same token, Jakes' procurement of millions in revenue from his books and videos should alert his followers that his motives for being in ministry are mixed with his appetite for affluence. With over thirty publications and seven yearly conferences, a critical onlooker will notice the redundancy of Jakes' messages in his many books and sermons. For example, after cornering the African American female Christian market with his first book, *Woman Thou Art Loosed*, Jakes has been targeting hurting women for years with more best-selling books, including *Daddy Loves His Girls*; *T.D. Jakes Speaks to Women*; *The Lady, Her Lover and Her Lord*; *His Lady: Sacred Promises for God's Woman*; and *God's Leading Lady*, as well as several accompanying workbooks. Careful scrutiny of this medium will expose streamlined themes and formulaic content that make the books almost indistinguishable.

Since Jakes must perpetuate wealth to keep his entrepreneurial machine going, he has not resisted offering new products with recycled themes from older books and videos. One is left to ponder if by targeting women Jakes is meeting needs or milking a cash cow? This query is especially salient in light of his professed role as a businessman because it is simply good business to target a market that will almost guarantee a great return on an investment.

Another example involves the evolution of ideas in his books. Though Jakes has never been dogmatic or particularly intolerant, his early books did make frequent allusions to many fundamentalist themes like spiritual warfare, Christ's atonement, Satan, the power of Jesus' blood, the spiritual gifts, speaking in tongues, judgment day, hell, sexual sins, and various other facets of his Pentecostal faith. After signing with the secular publishing giant Penguin Putnam, many of Jakes' books became increasingly secular or pluralistic by focusing less on sin, judgment, and holiness, and more on psychological truths and reliable godly aphorisms. LaVerne Chambers, a Chicago native and ardent supporter of Jakes' ministry, was so disappointed with his *Maximize the Moment* video series that she returned it and demanded her money back. Chambers complained that Jakes did not mention Jesus Christ's name once in the three videos, and that she could have easily purchased self-help videos from Les Brown if that was all she wanted.

Jakes' latest literary efforts include a novel and a Christmas book to expand his secular following. This transition toward a doctrineless, inoffensive gospel might be indicative of a standardized message that is palatable for many people so he can increase his market share. Such a transition is not surprising considering Jakes' postmodern style of ministry. As he continues to attract the mainstream media, Jakes will face tough questions concerning how far can he go in contextualizing his message and gifts for an expanding non-Christian audience without alienating his evangelical supporters.

Juanita Bynum

Jakes' numerous conferences generate millions in revenue through strategic marketing of the sermon videos of talented preachers as invited guests. In 2003, Jakes added his God's Leading Lady Conference Tour in stadiums of such cities as Jacksonville, Philadelphia, and Charlotte in addition to his three yearly events: Manpower, Woman Thou Art Loosed, and Pastors and Leadership Conference. He invites popular preachers and Christian entertainers, drawing thousands to each conference and producing large profits. Guest speakers and performers benefit by receiving generous stipends and added exposure. In return, Jakes generates millions of dollars by charging attendees for preferred seating and by retaining rights to videos and tapes of every speaker, which he markets on his television program and sells through his hotline.

Jakes' dealings with Juanita Bynum, a popular traveling evangelist, provide another example of a shaky convergence of business and ministry. When Bynum preached at his conference in 1998, Jakes made a fortune by selling many videos and tapes of her performance. The video's tremendous popularity and profitability led to a legal quarrel between Bynum and Jakes over royalties. Jakes responded by using his power and influence to have her blacklisted from preaching in many venues. A ministry insider with close ties to the Potter's House claimed that Jakes' efforts at blacklisting Bynum were intentional and thorough. This was confirmed by a staff member of a prominent church who revealed that during the legal dispute Jakes called her pastor and requested him not to invite Bynum for future conferences and engagements. This was also verified by an anonymous pastor in Memphis, who commented:

> Juanita Bynum thought she had the power to stand up to Jakes but didn't realize how truly powerful he is. Bynum had to preach at white churches because few large black churches would have her. But she developed new networks with white churches and stood on her own for some time and I respect her for that.

Jakes' and Bynum's mending process began in 2003 when she appeared on his television show as part of a reunion series for previous speakers at his conference. The fact that Bynum preached the most famous and best-selling sermon in his conference's history perhaps compelled Jakes to include her in the reunion in spite of their past dispute. At first Bynum appeared timid and uncomfortable, but by the end she was laughing and contented, demonstrating that the ice was broken between her and Jakes. A few months later, Bynum humbly apologized to Jakes at the Woman Thou Art Loosed 2003 conference, where she got down on her knees and pleaded for his forgiveness in front of tens of thousands of women in Houston's Reliant Stadium. She gave a passionate apology, claiming that God blocked opportunities for her to preach at prominent churches in order to rid her of pride; in fact, it was more likely that Jakes' blacklisting efforts produced her lesson in humility. Perhaps Bynum knew this but made a pragmatic choice to give the public apology and open the floodgates for new ministry opportunities. Her apology brought fruitful results by restoring invitations to keynote large conferences, including Jakes' Mega Fest convention in 2004. Currently, Bynum is back on track as one of the highest-paid traveling evangelists in the country. Jakes' treatment of Bynum demonstrates the type of Machiavellian politics powerful spiritual leaders employ to protect their empires.

Television Ministry

Another precarious nexus with Jakes as businessman and minister involves the symbiotic relationship between his for-profit endeavors and his national television ministry. As we have learned, televangelists establish an expansive mailing list of potential donors (usually called "partners") to defray the expenses of televising nationally, under the guise that their financial gifts will help these ministers reach millions of souls with the gospel. By employing scriptures and strategic phrases such as "Sow a Seed and Reap a Blessing," Jakes appeals to the spiritual consciousness of thousands of potential partners to provide the financial support necessary to defray the costs for broadcasting his show on national television. Here is an excerpt of a support letter I received from T.D. Jakes Ministries shortly after purchasing some books from his hotline:

Dear Shayne,

"And he said unto them, Go ye into all the world, and preach the gospel to every creature," Mark 16:15. Through your financial support of this ministry you are able to keep this charge given to us by our Lord and Savior, Jesus Christ. Your continued commitment will denote an invaluable pillar in the foundational structure of this great work. Your prompt response to this appeal will be immediately put to the task of empowering millions through the medium of television.

Here is an excerpt from the next letter I received a month later, soliciting support for Jakes' television ministry:

Through the outreach of The Potter's House and Potter's Touch broadcast we will send the message of redemption around the world, giving hope to our brothers and sisters in the Lord and a way of escape to the lost. Your support helps to make this possible. Take this opportunity to make a strong statement to the enemy regarding the victory that we know is ours. Sowing into the good ground of this ministry will make that statement and bring you a harvest in your time of need. There is no other investment for our future as sure as the promise of God's Word, "Give, and it shall be given unto you; good measure, pressed down, and shaken together, and running over, shall men give into your bosom. For with the same measure that ye mete withal it shall be measured to you again." Luke 6:38 KJV.

Jakes thus frames support for his television ministry in spiritual language urging his followers to help spread the gospel. As a result, thousands of people have joined Aaron's Army and the Bishop Circle, two groups of supporters giving a set amount of money to Jakes' ministry. Each member of Aaron's Army gives $20 a month or more and each member of the Bishop Circle gives an initial donation of $500 and a yearly gift of $1,000. Since donations from partners defray the costs of his national television ministry, Jakes does not have to pay out of his pocket for continual exposure and free marketing.

Rather than simply spreading the gospel, Jakes' television broadcasts double as infomercials to promote his movie, his forthcoming conferences, cruises, and the sale of his latest video or book. Every time Jakes preaches a new sermon series at his church or conference, he can be confident that through strategic marketing on his television broadcasts, it can procure him a fortune. For example, Jakes' program aired exciting clips of the sermon series *You Don't Have to Believe in My Dream* on every show for more than a month to tantalize listeners into purchasing the series. Jakes spends weeks broadcasting clips from previous Manpower and Woman Thou Art Loosed conferences to entice viewers to purchase the entire video series. Once the listener is hooked by the clips and is ready to buy, he can simply dial Jakes' twenty-four hour hotline and tell the customer-service attendant the name of the series he would like to purchase. The proceeds from the sale of videos, books, and Christian paraphernalia make Jakes very wealthy. Such a strategic use of the airwaves demonstrates how his television ministry is connected to his quest to expand his market share and sell millions of videos and books.

This is not to suggest that Jakes is the only preacher benefiting from free advertising and self-promotion through national broadcasts on Christian television. In our hypercapitalist postmodern age of technology, televangelism has fattened the portfolios of numerous preachers through the national exposure it generates. Television made Billy Graham a household name. Oral Roberts and Pat Robertson were able to sell millions of books through free marketing on their weekly broadcasts. More recently, Benny Hinn, Creflo Dollar, Kenneth Copeland, John Hagee, Paula White, Rod Parsley, Joel Osteen, Clarence McClendon, and a host of other preaching celebrities profit from their broadcasts and, accordingly, only few televangelists are not millionaires. Televangelism offers strategic opportunities and exposure that are far too profitable for Jakes and others to ignore. TBN receives close to $200 million in annual revenues by selling time slots to celebrity preachers. But no ministry has been nearly as savvy in coordinating symmetry between a nonprofit television ministry and for-profit entrepreneurial activity as Jakes.

Pastoral Partiality

The convergence of businessman and minister can also be seen in Jakes' pastoral duties as shepherd to a flock of 28,000 members of the Potter's House. A demanding schedule prevents Jakes from conferring individual attention on almost all of his members, as even staff and friends voiced frustration about their lack of personal time with Jakes. Jakes' large membership understandably causes him to function more like a statesman than a shepherd. One woman disclosed that after three years of membership, "I still haven't met Bishop Jakes face-to-face." It is therefore perplexing how Jakes finds the time to give individual attention to new celebrity members of his church.

For example, Dallas Cowboys superstar Deion Sanders met Jakes when Sanders and his wife went to Jakes for marriage counseling. One may wonder how Deion Sanders and his now ex-wife gained access to individual marriage counseling from Jakes as new members, since he did not afford the same opportunity to most of the others in his flock. Sanders had a dramatic conversion experience, after which Jakes became his spiritual mentor. Shortly after, Sanders preached at crusades with Jakes, and now he affectionately refers to Jakes as "Daddy." It is appropriate to ask if any noncelebrity preaching protégés of the Potter's House were able to accompany Jakes on preaching crusades. Mentoring the football star proved to be good business in 1998, when Sanders gave a million-dollar donation to the Potter's House.

Deion Sanders is not the only troubled athlete who has received personal attention from Jakes. Former Dallas Cowboys superstar, Michael Irvin, had trouble with the law in the summer of 2000 when he was arrested on a drug charge that was later dismissed. Irvin's bouts with drugs and prostitution placed a strain on his marriage and public image until he became a Christian and had a personal relationship with Jakes. Like Sanders, Irvin spent time traveling with Jakes and claims their relationship helped alleviate depression in his life. Irvin's association with Jakes also restored the former football star's tattered public image. In a 2002 interview on the television show *Best Damn Sports Show Period*, the controversial boxer Mike Tyson recalled how Irvin used to be "crazier than me until he began hanging with T.D. Jakes." The fact that Irvin and Sanders were given immediate access to Jakes for individual counseling and mentoring may be troubling to thousands of members of the Potter's House who can't get close enough to shake their pastor's hand. Similarly, some members complained to me that the Potter's House offers preferred seating to celebrities and VIPs.

Paying tens of thousands of dollars in property taxes on his $2 million home each year, in addition to the expenses involved in maintaining a private jet, a fleet of expensive cars, and a first-class lifestyle motivates Jakes to generate large sums of personal income by finding new ways to commercialize Christianity. He can no longer afford to take respites for fasting and spiritual replenishment because his empire depends on the production of books, speaking engagements, and entrepreneurial activity at a steady pace. Jakes must also preach at the largest and most wealthy churches and conferences that can afford his exorbitant honorarium rather than choosing his speaking engagements "as the Spirit leads," so to speak. Hence, Jakes' pursuit of the American dream may be losing him the prophetic edge.

Jakes the entrepreneur produces a profusion of books, tapes, CDs, videos, plays, and commercial items to clients who yearn to hear words of wisdom from Jakes, the anointed man of God. This recurrent dance from minister to businessman is important because it allows Jakes to justify his opulent lifestyle and capitalistic empire, claiming they are a result of God blessing his businesses. At the same time, he constantly underemphasizes the fact that he is in the business of selling God. The demands of maintaining a vast entrepreneurial machine forces Jakes to make crafty decisions to generate the necessary resources to support large staffs, creative marketing initiatives, and produce products that have mass appeal.

I have written much about Jakes being part of a faith industry that produces spiritual commodities for mass consumption. But mass consumption demands the securing of many clients, which means standardizing religious products to meet the needs and tastes of the American masses. Jakes is under pressure to keep his machine going and therefore cannot afford to offend too many people. In this way, his strength is his greatest source of criticism: the ability to contextualize Christianity to fit the existential cravings of many Americans. Rodney Sadler, a professor of religion, claimed that preachers like Jakes "represent an easy kind of Christianity" that focuses on how God will bless you instead of emphasizing the sacrifices demanded by the kingdom of God on your life. Similarly, religion scholar Brad Braxton commented:

> To be sure, the Christian gospel speaks to needs but whenever needs and the addressing of needs is the only message that we hear, are we not offering an emaciated or truncated gospel? Sometimes the gospel doesn't address our problems, sometimes the gospel creates problems. That's the piece that's missing, maybe in Jakes, maybe in these word of faith preachers. Everything is always solutions, solutions, solutions. (Interview)

Many supporters buy his products because they are addressing needs, but many critics argue that Jakes offers a watered-down gospel by conforming to the contemporary tides of American culture.

Commercializing religion did not begin with Jakes; religion has always functioned as a collectively produced entity and its products have been bought and sold for millennia. Whether it was African Shamans and Israelite Levites of antiquity, or Baptist preachers and Catholic clerics of today, the labor responsible for the spiritual needs of people has always received remuneration. But an important principle concerning the compensation of religious services is that clergy seem to have more credibility when they obtain fewer material rewards. Mahatma Gandhi and Martin Luther King Jr. are less controversial in this regard; they never became rich from their altruistic endeavors, but rather they chose to live more moderately than Jakes and many contemporary preachers. Jakes' blend of business and spirituality represents a postmodern feature of contemporary American religion in which the lines between the secular and spiritual are increasingly blurred.

T.D. Jakes is the small-town boy who reinvented himself to make it in the big city. He is also a larger-than-life capitalist building an empire using religion as his most valuable commodity. Jakes succumbs to the materialistic seductions of our consumer culture, and his blend of spirituality and capitalism awakens questions about our nation's moral and spiritual direction. Shrewd businessman and compassionate preacher are equally salient aspects of his personal identity. His ministry is saving souls, and his businesses are prospering off those souls. Like music pop star Britney Spears and basketball sensation Michael Jordan, Jakes and many popular preachers are products of a technological age of hype and simulation that transforms celebrities into valuable commodities. The emergence of this new age of million-dollar preachers and mega churches is part of a neo-Pentecostal revolution that many will soon learn to perceive as the new black church.

[8]

The New Black Church

> The conservative traditional mainline churches are in an uproar because they can't compete because they're so stuck in tradition and so uncreative and unimaginative as preachers that they are totally unwilling to make the kind of necessary shift they need in order to compete with this market that T.D. Jakes and the new black church have put their fingers on.
> —Renita Weems

What do Eddie Long, Paul Morton, and T.D. Jakes have in common? They are prominent black pastors of churches exceeding 20,000 members. Long, Morton, Jakes, and many other celebrity pastors demonstrate that we have approached a new era in American Protestantism where neo-Pentecostal mega churches represent the greatest challenge the traditional black church has ever faced. More shocking than Jakes' appearance on the cover of *Time* magazine's September 17, 2001, issue was the fact that *Time* asked if a neo-Pentecostal preacher is the next American religious icon. This was a powerful indicator that neo-Pentecostalism has become a force in American religion, with Jakes as its greatest superstar. It was a neo-Pentecostal media takeover that established the broadcast structure for Jakes' dramatic rise. Now he thrives as the primary figure behind a new Protestant landscape that continues to blur denominational lines with new networks and mega churches large enough to operate as their own spiritual movements.

The church, like any institution, grows, changes, and develops over periods of time. Religious organizations create, maintain, and supply religion to segments of people and supervise their exchanges with God (Stark and Finke 2000). When the leading religious groups underperform in meeting the needs of a particular segment of the population, the opportunity emerges for new movements to transform fundamental conceptions of religion and spirituality. For example, the predominant roles enjoyed by Congregationalists and Episcopalians in the eighteenth century were lost to Methodists and Baptists in the nineteenth century, whose messages and ministries resonated more with common people. Similarly, for much of the last hundred years, it was pastors from the National Baptist Convention (NBC) and the African Methodist Episcopal (AME) Church who competed as the primary figures and predominant spokespersons for the black church. As the first black denomination and the largest black denomination, respectively, the AME Church and the NBC enjoyed prominent places in the black community and produced many African American leaders of the past two centuries.

But today's postdenominational religious landscape contains a host of black neo-Pentecostal preachers who have built mega churches and national ministries as part of the emergence of what I have coined the new black church. These celebrity preachers are CEOs of international ministries that reach millions of people through television, radio, the Internet, and by satellite technology, and their churches have resources rivaling denominations. These pastors take advantage of our media age by marketing their books, videos, and tapes to secure personal fortunes. These spiritual leaders compete for twenty-first-century souls among a growing black middle class and newly educated African Americans excelling in corporate America, a niche that has intriguing possibilities.

Black mega churches are not entirely new. Black churches had been the predominant institutions of the black community for a long time, and the fact that some of them have exploded in membership is not surprising. Since preaching was one of few progressive career options for many African Americans, blacks have always been oversaturated with churches, some of which have grown to large memberships. Some scholars may argue that Jakes and his contemporaries are therefore not doing anything new. But the notion of a new black church sheds light on a shift that most researchers tend to miss in the context of contemporary black religion, which, taken together, can very well be called a "new" form in the legacy of the black church. In the last thirty years the trend has been for traditional mainline churches to lose their prominent places in the market share to neo-Pentecostal churches, which have secured phenomenal growth because they encompass many of the trends in American popular religion.

Women in Ministry

One trait that distinguishes Jakes and the new black church is a greater acceptance of female pastors and preachers. While mainline denominations continue to debate over the Bible's position on women in ministry, neo-Pentecostal mega churches nationwide are welcoming women in their pulpits and giving female preachers unprecedented support. The Full Gospel Baptist Church Fellowship has been the most vocal of all neo-Pentecostal networks in promoting women in church leadership by including this position as one of the tenets of its constitution. In the face of mainline black Baptist conventions that are generally hostile to women preachers, the Full Gospel Baptist Church Fellowship has adopted an aggressive egalitarian vision for women clergy.

Jackie McCullough, the female pastor of a thriving church in New York, maintains a hectic schedule as one of the most popular African American preachers in the country. McCullough has been able to transcend denominational lines by preaching in diverse contexts in some of the largest churches in the country. Carlton Pearson invited her to keynote the AZUSA Conference in its heyday, and Jakes recently proclaimed in a staff meeting that she is one of a few preachers in the country that can minister to him anytime. A few years ago McCullough made history as the first black female to keynote the Hampton Ministers and Music Conference—the exclusive old boys' network for prominent black preachers.

Ernestine Reems is a bishop in a small network of churches, and she mentors prominent pastors like Jakes. Juanita Bynum now preaches on TBN as a rising star whose candid discussions on sex and self-respect have reached the hearts of millions of Christians. Barbara Amos, pastor of a growing church in Virginia, preaches fiery sermons blending spirituality with an emphasis on black cultural consciousness. Johnnie Colemon pastors a 15,000-member church in Chicago. Vanessa Weatherspoon, Vashti McKenzie, Audrey Turner, Bridget Hilliard, Iona Locke, Wanda Turner, Brenda Little, Suzan Johnson Cook, Paulette Scott, Betty Peebles, and Wilma Johnson demonstrate that female preachers are engaged in a revolutionary struggle to play prominent roles in the new black church.

Many neo-Pentecostal pastors, such as Roderick Caesar of Bethel Gospel Tabernacle in New York City, ordain women to ministry and appoint them as associate pastors. In addition, a growing number of neo-Pentecostal mega churches are led by husband-and-wife pastoral teams. Courtney and Janeen McBath co-pastor the seven-thousand-member nondenominational Calvary Revival Church in Norfolk, which has been one of the fastest-growing in Virginia since its inception in 1990. Suzie and Alfred Owens co-pastor Greater Mount Calvary Holy Church, a popular church in Washington, D.C., with over six thousand members. Ira and Bridget Hilliard co-pastor New Light Christian Center Church in Houston, which claims 20,000 members. Michael and Dee Dee Freeman co-pastor Spirit of Faith Christian Center in Maryland, and their entire pastoral staff consists of eight husband-and-wife teams. Many more examples demonstrate this trend of team leadership in the new black church.

This is not to suggest that the new black church is completely egalitarian. Like Jakes, many neo-Pentecostals have complex and at times contradictory positions on women. Only a small proportion of black mega churches have women as senior pastors, and some, like Salem Baptist Church in Chicago, exclude women from preaching behind the pulpit. Even among Full Gospel Baptists where women clergy are most prevalent, only men participate in their state, regional, and national bishoprics. This demonstrates that the new black church has a long way to go before gender equality is fully achieved. But compared to the persistently patriarchal traditional black church, neo-Pentecostals stand in stark contrast by opening doors for women in ministry that were sealed for centuries.

Iconoclastic Preaching

Former governor of Vermont Howard Dean became an early front runner for the democratic presidential nomination after he positioned himself as an outsider of the political establishment. Dean's attack on the political status quo resonated with many disgruntled Democrats who felt powerless and voiceless during the first three years of President Bush's administration. Similarly, the new black church has a fondness for challenging everything it perceives as wrong with Grandma's religion and positions itself as an antipode to the old religious establishment. Many neo-Pentecostal preachers project strong antiestablishment feelings, suggesting fundamental change is needed in the church to address contemporary needs.

A central theme in the new black church is the disdain for religiosity, denominationalism, and traditionalism. The religious climate of the 1990s inspired Carlton Pearson, Paul Morton, Eddie Long, and other black neo-Pentecostal leaders to start new fellowships and conferences. These leaders appealed to a new generation of young black Christians experiencing problems with age hierarchy and traditionalism in the mainline denominations.

These leaders founded their churches, fellowships, and networks as movements amenable to change, as movements that embrace women in ministry, and as movements that embody a professional, technologically advanced, media-savvy coterie of neo-Pentecostals, as opposed to what they perceived as a backward black church.

Neo-Pentecostalism is as much a reaction against the legalism of classical Pentecostalism as it is against the formalism of mainline Baptists, Methodists, and Episcopalians. Traditionally, Pentecostals have enforced strict moral and dress codes and portray worldly pleasures as enmity against God. Neo-Pentecostals borrow Pentecostals' emphasis on the Holy Spirit but offer a religion that is more empowering and less stifling. They affirm an enjoyable spiritual experience and embrace worldly things that many classical Pentecostals eschew, such as movies, plays, secular music, financial prosperity, emotional and psychological well-being, and first-class lifestyles.

Neo-Pentecostal preachers position themselves as outsiders to the religious establishment, as enemies of religion and tradition, and as iconoclasts offering a new and vibrant religious experience. This is attractive to many Christians who have been disgruntled with the church. As a reaction against both the secularization and formalism of mainline churches, and the legalism and otherworldliness of Pentecostalism, neo-Pentecostals carve out an intriguing niche for themselves and have gotten many people excited about church again. By deemphasizing denominational affiliation, the new black church can cast a wider net and draw people from various backgrounds and traditions.

Personal Empowerment

When David Martin, a noted sociologist of religion, contended there is an affinity between neo-Pentecostalism and postmodernism (Martin 2002), he was not implying that neo-Pentecostals reject objective truth and deconstruct all forms of reality like many postmodern scholars, but was rather alluding to how neo-Pentecostals put less emphasis on doctrinal constraints and more weight on subjective experience. Jakes and neo-Pentecostals are postmodern in the sense that they emphasize personal empower-ment and the ability for the Holy Spirit to guide individuals in their daily lives. Such an approach authorizes members to depend less on religious elites and more on personal encounters with God through prayer and a radical daily devotional life. Dogma takes a back seat to seeking guidance from the Holy Spirit for one's daily experiences.

Neo-Pentecostals' radical emphasis on the believer's control of his or her destiny resonates in our age of pop psychology, motiva-tional tapes, and self-help books. Neo-Pentecostal preachers en-courage members to create their own spiritual breakthroughs by confessing scriptures and believing in God's promises, rather than conforming to firmly established church traditions. Jakes and the new black church offer an empowering religion that challenges Christians to "maximize the moment" or seize the day. By build-ing up their faith and "calling forth things that are not as though they were," neo-Pentecostals believe they have the power to change their circumstances.

Many black mega churches offer empowerment seminars in which business strategies are combined with spiritual principles to teach Christians how to attain first-class lifestyles. Some preachers are so bold as to suggest that Christians who have great faith are impervious to evil and can commission angels to protect their family. Neo-Pentecostals' emphasis on personal empowerment and individuality resonates in an increasingly postmodern society.

Music

Another element of the new black church involves innovative changes in Christian music. Neo-Pentecostals embrace recent innovations in secular music and use sensual lyrics and high-tech wizardry in captivating the attention of a generation raised on R&B music. Jakes, BeBe & CeCe Winans, Fred Hammond, and Kirk Franklin bring unprecedented exposure to gospel music at political conventions, television performances, world tours, and multiplatinum CD sales. Gospel artists' highly contemporary rhythm tracks present an important crossroads concerning the direction of Christian music. Some traditionalists contend that Christian artists have gone too far by trading in spirituality for secular appeal, and in its place hold steadfast to a traditional approach to gospel music. Conversely, most black neo-Pentecostal mega churches embrace contemporary changes in music that are attractive to many people who normally would not frequent churches.

Church historian David Daniels argues that many black Baptist churches have locked themselves into a mid-twentieth-century church culture that impedes them from competing with the vibrant music pervading neo-Pentecostal churches nationwide. The result, Daniels contends, is that those churches that are able to adjust to changes in music are still thriving while the others are in decline (Morris and Lee 2005). Chicago, like most cities nationwide, has churches that illustrate Daniels' point. Churches like Pilgrim Baptist Church and Olivet Baptist Church continue to play older music styles and sing traditional hymns and anthems. Though they drew thousands of members a few decades ago, Pilgrim and Olivet are now lucky to see a few hundred members on Sunday, thus demonstrating what can happen to prominent churches in a competitive religious marketplace when the environment changes and they do not. Conversely, new churches in the Chicago area like Salem Baptist Church and Valley Kingdom experienced explosive growth after their church services used contemporary Christian music and embraced the neo-Pentecostal worship experience.

Praise and Worship

If one were to visit Windsor Village in Houston one week and then West Angeles Church of God in Christ in Los Angeles the following Sunday, one would encounter similar worship experiences. In each church, one would hear praise teams leading congregants in worship songs and praise dancers gliding through the aisles, and visible displays of worship from members. Windsor Village is part of the United Methodist Church and West Angeles is part of the Church of God in Christ—two denominations that are starkly different. Yet both churches provide almost indistinguishable worship experiences because they have veered from the course of their traditional denominations to exude a neo-Pentecostal style of praise and worship.

Neo-Pentecostalism brought sweeping changes to many black churches in past decades, namely, an emphasis on worshiping God and experiencing the power of the Holy Spirit. The emotional release from dramatic episodes of unrestricted praise and worship has a cathartic effect that has made it increasingly difficult for traditional churches to compete for market share. In their monumental study on the black church, C. Eric Lincoln and Lawrence Mamiya distinguished neo-Pentecostalism's effect:

> Neo-Pentecostalism in black churches tends to draw upon the reservoir of the black folk religious tradition which stressed enthusiastic worship and Spirit filled experiences. One of the appeals of the current movement is its emphasis upon a deeper spirituality, the need for a second blessing of the Holy Spirit. (Lincoln and Mamiya 1990:386)

Lincoln and Mamiya acknowledged that the fastest-growing churches in black mainline denominations are neo-Pentecostal, which they argued continue to threaten church growth in traditional black mainline churches:

The challenge which neo-Pentecostalism poses for the Black Church is real, and the issue of how to benefit from this potential of church growth and spiritual revitalization without alienating the pillars of normative tradition . . . and without producing a crisis of schism is a challenge most black churches must inevitably address. (Ibid.:388)

Many traditional black Baptist and Methodist churches have structured devotions in which a deacon or other member leads the congregation in solemn hymns followed by a few songs from the choir, whereas neo-Pentecostals have longer times of "praise and worship" led by praise teams of specially trained singers who help "usher in the presence of the Holy Spirit," so to speak. Neo-Pentecostal praise and worship, exemplified by singing, dancing, and other ecstatic expressions, can last anywhere from thirty minutes to an hour. Neo-Pentecostals also teach beliefs and practices that are often in tension with traditional mainliners.

Neo-Pentecostal praise and worship is often a complicated endeavor combining Old Testament emphases on Tabernacle worship and priestly duties with a New Testament focus on the gifts of the Holy Spirit. Walter Owens, a musicologist and worship leader at Salem Baptist Church in Chicago, added:

Praise and worship reduced to its simplest terms is acknowledgment of God, acknowledgment of His works, speaking of Him, singing about Him; we have just in the last probably ten years come to understand what the Bible says about it and so we highlight scripture and we now call it praise and worship. (Interview)

Praise leaders often introduce songs with Hebrew concepts from the Old Testament such as *Shabach*, *Barak*, and *Tehillah* that demonstrate compelling expressions of worship to God. Praise leaders also teach participants to offer visible expressions of praise and adoration, including raising their arms as a sign of surrender to God, whereas traditional mainline devotions are more constrained. Praise leaders persuade their members not to be mere spectators but rather active participants in preparing the congregation for God's manifested presence.

Neo-Pentecostal praise and worship sessions evoke the kind of passion that makes participants feel they are connecting with God. Fervent spiritual experiences inspire members to reach beyond the levels of creed and ceremony into the depths of human emotion (Cox 2001). Worship leaders are like spiritual coaches urging their listeners to dig deeper and reach further to offer God unadulterated praise. Talented musicians play in the background while congregants sing worship songs that were written with the purpose of inspiring intense devotion to God. By providing a similar blueprint for worship, neo-Pentecostalism is blurring denominational lines as a postmodern movement of spirituality.

Celebrity Preachers

Another feature of the new black church involves the unprecedented celebrity of many of its leaders. This is not to minimize the historical leadership role black pastors played in the civic life of their communities. But the acclaim that neo-Pentecostals are receiving is a more recent phenomenon due to televangelism, widespread marketing of books, videos, CDs, and the power many of them wield as "CEOs" of institutions with thousands of members. Preachers like Jakes have social capital in popular culture as never before, and gospel artists like Kirk Franklin are competing with secular music stars in popularity and album sales. Similarly, there are examples in cities nationwide of African American pastors of neo-Pentecostal mega churches who have become virtual celebrities.

Donnie McClurkin, gospel artist and pastor of Perfecting Faith in Freeport, Long Island, wrote musical scores for a major Disney movie, has been a celebrity guest on Black Entertainment Television, and was a featured singer at the 2004 Republican National Convention. Creflo Dollar recently appeared in a hip-hop music video profiling Atlanta celebrities. Charles Blake received millions of dollars from basketball legend Magic Johnson and Academy Award–winning actor Denzel Washington to build West Angeles Cathedral, a $60 million worship center that has become a landmark in Los Angeles. Juanita Bynum has been a keynote speaker for *Essence* magazine's yearly music festivals and is adored by several pop stars, including R&B singer Mary J. Blige. James Meeks, a pastor of an 18,000-member neo-Pentecostal Baptist church in Chicago, frequently appears on CNN and mentors the controversial music star R. Kelly. Keith Butler in Detroit, Jackie McCullough in New York, Eddie Long in Atlanta, and various other black neo-Pentecostal preachers also enjoy unprecedented infusion into pop culture.

Whether it is in the world of movie stars, musicians, athletes, or preachers, celebrity does attract its imitators. Young women want to wear the clothes that pop icons Britney Spears and Beyonce wear, and young athletes want to be like Maria Sharapova and Le-Bron James because people want to look like celebrities and vicariously share in their successes. Similarly, "The religious marketplace, although one may want to see it as separate, shares in the dynamics of the secular world and often those presenting images of success attract imitators," claimed Larry Murphy, a noted scholar of religion in an interview. Murphy discussed how neo-Pentecostal preachers create an aura of celebrity by flying across the country in private jets and traveling with security entourages similar to those of politicians and movie stars. Murphy added that congregants who see their pastors on television, read their latest books, and take in their celebrity and influence are proud to associate with them. Their celebrity in return creates a buzz that draws more curious members to visit and attend their churches.

There are Jakes clones all over the country who imitate his flashy image and preaching style, shouting catchy phrases like,

"Get ready, get ready, get ready!" Many young pastors imitate neo-Pentecostals like Jakes and Paul Morton because their large ministries are perceived as successful. Preachers who drive fancy cars and live in multimillion-dollar homes represent values that are attractive and compelling for many Christians acculturated into the American way of life. David Butler, a pastor in Queens New York, noted:

> I think a lot of churches have brought into the model that their success is driven by standards that are not necessarily spiritual. How many members you have, how much money you're bringing in, what kind of car you drive, how many jets do you have? I take exception to that kind of mentality. If they were to judge Jesus by the number of people who really believed in him then he might not meet their standards. (Interview)

Neo-Pentecostal preachers often become contemporary success models that other pastors and members can imitate, and in return they garner even more popularity.

Their increasing celebrity is causing a new movement some have coined "one church, two locations," in which several pastors of neo-Pentecostal mega churches are popular enough to hold worship services in different locations under the umbrella of one church. In this way, one person can travel back and forth as the pastor of what amounts to two different churches and use the same nonprofit organizational structure, ministry name, board of trustees, and so on. Larry Trotter pastors Sweet Holy Spirit Full Gospel Baptist Church, which meets every Sunday in two locations in South Chicago. Donald Shorter pastors Pacific Christian Center Church in two locations in the adjacent cities of Tacoma, Washington, and Portland, Oregon. Donald Hilliard pastors Cathedral International, which has three locations in adjacent cities in New Jersey. Paul Morton pastors Greater St. Stephen Full Gospel Baptist Church, which now has three separate locations offering eight worship services per week in New Orleans and the surrounding area. Ira and Bridget Hilliard pastor New Light Christian Center Church and travel in their private helicopter to conduct separate services each Sunday in North Houston and Southwest Houston. Claude Alexander pastors University Park Baptist Church, which has two locations in Charlotte, North Carolina. Michael and Dee Dee Freeman co-pastor Spirit of Faith Christian Center in two separate locations in northern and southern Maryland. Hezekiah Walker pastors Love Fellowship Tabernacle in Brooklyn, New York, and Willingboro, New Jersey. And surprisingly, Fred Price pastors one church in two locations on opposite coasts—in California and New York—and flies back and forth in his Lear jet. Conducting services in separate locations gives pastors increased exposure and power in their cities.

Pastors in the new black church also live like celebrities. It would be very difficult to find a televangelist or pastor with over eight thousand members who is not a millionaire. The pervasive prosperity gospel has created a landscape that justifies their exorbitant speaking fees and salaries that resemble those of CEOs of a large corporation. These pastors travel in private jets, live in posh neighborhoods, drive fleets of luxury cars, and send their children to elite private schools.

A drawback of celebrity is that it causes pastors to function as untouchable statesmen rather than shepherds of their flock, as encouraged in the New Testament. Most members of the Potter's House in Dallas will never have a one-on-one meeting with T.D. Jakes. Eddie Long more than likely cannot be called on to bail out from jail the troubled son of one of his 21,000 members. Most members of Faithful Central Bible Church in Inglewood, California, will never receive personal counseling from their celebrity pastor, Kenneth Ulmer. Similarly, most congregants of Full Harvest International in Los Angeles, Greater Allen Cathedral in New York, and Redemptive Life Fellowship in West Palm Beach will never receive personal attention from their respective pastors Clarence McClendon, Floyd Flake, and Harold Ray. Personal celebrity invites death threats and enemies, and as a precaution many pastors preach their sermons and fade away with a smile like the Cheshire Cat rather than interacting with members after services.

Professionalism and Technology

We are in a postmodern age with advanced technology, new wealth, new commercial networks, and new methods of delivering information. Social critics of the past such as Max Weber and Auguste Comte predicted that as societies become more technologically sophisticated, religion would face a tremendous decline in influence. Their secularization thesis contends that in response to modernization, religious institutions, actions, and consciousness will lose their social significance (Stark and Finke 2000). The new black church shatters their long-held prediction.

A salient feature of many neo-Pentecostal mega churches involves incorporating technology and professionalism into people's social and spiritual experiences. The mixing of codes from religion with elements of contemporary and secular culture is at the heart of the success of Jakes and the new black church. Neo-Pentecostals like Jakes blend fervent spirituality with sophisticated business acumen. Not only do they market books, videos, CDs, and plays, and use satellite technology to broadcast sermons all across the nation, but a growing number are using video clips and computer graphics in their services and are building large organizational infrastructures that meet secular needs in the community.

Windsor Village may be the prototypical new black church in this regard. Kirbyjon Caldwell became the senior pastor in 1982 when the church had fewer than thirty members, and now it is the largest United Methodist Church in the country. Windsor Village is a force in Houston: it runs nine separate organizations that make up what members call the Power Connection. A central part of the Power Connection is the Pyramid Community Development Corporation, which consists of a multiuse complex, bank, community college, office suites, a pharmacy, and a conference center. Windsor Village also runs several other nonprofit organizations and holds empowerment seminars and power lunches attended by business executives of large corporations.

Evangel Fellowship, a mega church in Greensboro, North Carolina, has Sunday School courses on an array of topics that provide spiritual and practical insight by trained business professionals. Evangel's senior pastor, Otis Lockett, discussed his church's vision:

> The whole vision of our ministry is to provide biblical solutions to promote personal success: life, family and work. That's the whole gist of it all. Success is knowing God, what he desires for my life, growing to my maximum potential and sowing seeds that would benefit others. (Interview)

Lockett's goal is to blend the spiritual fervency of Pentecostalism with pragmatic training that addresses relevant needs:

> I saw the spiritual part of Pentecostalism, you know, the embracing of the Holy Spirit, the gifts of the Spirit, the laying on of hands, the emotionalism that accompanies worship, and I really felt a great need to teach people. One of the basic premises of my life is if it's not practical then it's not spiritual and so I've always tried to do things that were practical, things that were relevant. That's how we've come around to do classes on business ethics, how to start a business, how to get the promotions, classes on marriage; I'm a very need-conscious person. (Ibid.)

In addition to preaching a message of material well-being, Lockett and other progressive black pastors pride themselves in running their churches like businesses and for utilizing the latest technology to address the needs of their large followings.

As part of a new trend among black mega churches, New Birth Missionary Baptist Church in Atlanta operates a magazine and sells videos of church services through an elaborate 3-D Website. Less than twenty miles away is another church in College Park called World Changers Ministries, which owns a music studio, publishing house, and record label. James Meeks, pastor of Salem Baptist Church on Chicago's South Side, claims his church was the first in the country to broadcast live services on the Internet, and Salem now owns the largest Christian bookstore in Chicago. University Park Baptist Church in Charlotte, North Carolina, has an elaborate online bookstore and offers a live Web cast of each Sunday service. Faithful Central Bible Church, a 12,000 member congregation in Inglewood, California, recently purchased the Great Western Forum from the NBA basketball team, the Los Angeles Lakers. Redemptive Life Fellowship in West Palm Beach, Florida, has several for-profit corporations, including a clothing business, travel agency, and a real estate company. Abundant Life Cathedral in Houston has high-tech television and audio equipment, a color-changeable sky backdrop, a record company, and a distribution service for sermon messages on DVD. Greater Allen Cathedral in Queens, New York, operates various commercial and social service enterprises that employ an eight-hundred-person workforce. Pacific Christian Center in Tacoma, Washington, offers free business seminars and professional workshops.

Like the politicians who are using new media to bring thousands of new people into the political process, Jakes and the new black church use new media and technology to bring thousands of new people into the church. More and more neo-Pentecostal mega churches are utilizing expansive mailing lists, displaying announcements and dramatizations on large video screens, owning large Christian bookstores, and running live Web casts and sophisticated Web sites that allow members to post prayers and donate money. Their prosperity teachings encourage members to give liberal offerings to the church, which helps them accumulate capital for business ventures and splurge on state-of-the-art equipment. The prosperity ideology also justifies these pastors' luxurious cars, expensive clothes, and posh lifestyles: very few leaders in the new black church are not fabulously wealthy.

The new black church demonstrates that we may be approaching an era in which lines of demarcation between the secular and spiritual world become increasingly blurred. Some, like theologian Dwight Hopkins, justifiably argue that integrating the secular with the spiritual is part of the African and slave heritage and so it is in fact as much a return to old ways as it is a recent phenomenon (Hopkins 2003). Rather than facing a decline, as social thinkers of the past had predicted, religion in the twenty-first century will see mega churches increasing their market share by addressing problems traditionally answered by secular institutions. This is not to overlook the historic institutional centrality of the traditional black church and the breadth of the extrareligious traditions it has embodied. But the new black church is armed with greater professional resources, skills, and technology than ever before, drawing new people who traditionally utilized secular organizations to address their existential needs. An African American who needs a travel agent, bookstore, record label, business loan, conference center, hotel room, theatrical production, empowerment seminar, business training, and so on, is increasingly more likely to patronize the services of one of the neo-Pentecostal mega churches in his city.

Jakes is the metaphor of a new black church that energizes audiences with ecstatic worship experiences, lively music, and prosperity preaching. Jakes and the new black church are business savvy, culture affirming, and peculiarly American. Jakes and the new black church utilize state-of-the-art technology and continue to blur denominational lines. What distinguishes Jakes and the new black church is their ability to offer a vibrant otherworldly worship experience and a this-worldly message and ministry.

Many white neo-Pentecostal churches have several features in common with Jakes and the new black church. A growing number of spiritual leaders like Tommy Barnett, pastor of an 18,000 member church in Arizona, blend contemporary developments in technology and culture with practical spiritual messages to reach a sight-and-sound generation. More and more clerics, like Joel Osteen, pastor of Lakewood Church, a 25,000-member congregation in Texas, preach practical messages addressing the existential cravings of contemporary Americans. A growing number of ministers, like Casey Treat, pastor of Christian Faith Center in Washington state, are preaching economic prosperity and holding seminars designed for business people. The rise of mega churches demonstrates that we have reached an era in American religion where the more versatile, professional, and business-savvy that churches are, the more competitive they can be in the religious marketplace.

It is ironic that Pentecostalism, the branch of Christendom that once harbored ardent antisecular sentiment, transformed into a neo-Pentecostal movement with the strongest embrace of technology, secularism, capitalism, and popular culture. Jakes and the new black church are thriving because they are postmodern and they address the cultural tastes and existential thirsts of contemporary American society. These ministries emphasize the therapeutic benefits of the faith and offer an optimistic view of the future that embraces American ideals of prosperity. In our competitive religious landscape, churches that adjust to cultural changes are flourishing while traditional churches lag behind and lose many members.

Many ask whether this thriving postmodern church reflects a permanent shift in American religion or if it is just a fad. This leads us to wonder if the Potter's House will survive beyond Jakes. And will Lakewood Church's demise begin with the departure of Joel Osteen? Will Creflo Dollar, Bill Hybels, Edwin Young, Eddie Long, Paul Morton, Rick Warren, and other celebrity pastors of mega churches transform their charisma into durable institutions that will endure after their deaths, or will their large congregations expire with them? The resilience of these high-tech, culture-affirming, business-savvy religious suppliers will depend on their ability to continue addressing the needs and appetites of their clients.

Because consumer preferences differ, the American religious marketplace can never be successfully monopolized (Finke and Stark 1992). There are many Christians whose feet will never touch the ground of a mega church, and some Christians will cling to Grandma's religion until death. Hence, there will always be a place for smaller traditional Protestant churches, and the trade-offs made by large ministries may one day ignite an exodus of disgruntled members. However, the current popularity of mega churches leads us to believe the small-church-on-the-corner niche is dramatically declining in the American religious market-place. Small neighborhood churches are finding it increasingly difficult to compete with larger ones that offer more choices under one roof.

Whether or not this trend is detrimental to Christendom is a question I will leave in the hands of theologians, apologists, spiritual leaders, and the countless nameless faces that attend churches nationwide. Much more can be discussed about the challenges and drawbacks of mega churches, as well as the many moral considerations involved with the commercialization of spirituality for personal gain. Hopefully scholars and journalists will continue to explore how celebrity preachers surf the wave of this neo-Pentecostal revolution to become religious icons and how their messages and ministries will affect society in years to come.

American Phenomenon

Summary and Conclusion

> The American phenomenon is one of being able to exploit
> your talent in the marketplace for as much currency as the
> market will bear. That's the foundation of a market economy
> and that's what distinguishes Jakes' American gospel. It is a
> gospel of personal agency and a gospel of prosperity rooted
> in American ideals.   —Travis Lee

The early American sojourners found themselves without much
of a blueprint and thus had to carve out their own niche to meet
the demands of the moment. Consequently, America cherished
the heroic attempt of self-creation and became a nation characterized by a faith in simple dreams and an insistence on small mira-
cles. In the words of Barack Obama, the son of a Kenyan goat
herder and a white American mother, who recently was elected a
U.S. senator, "In no other country on earth is my story possible."
America is the type of setting where a former slave like Booker T.
Washington could become a national leader, and a poor boxer
like Joe Frazier could rise above the rough streets of Philadelphia
to become a world champion. It is also the kind of place where a
country preacher from West Virginia was able to transcend
poverty and become a legend.

Jakes grew up in the hills of West Virginia as the youngest child
in an enterprising family. His early dichotomy as "Bible Boy"
preaching sermons to the wind and as pesky peddler of vegetables

and Avon products reveals that businessman and preacher are equally salient aspects of his personal identity. Today we can see Jakes selling videos with the same tenacity in which he sold fish from his father's truck as a diligent boy. At a young age, Jakes learned how to console the brokenhearted through family tragedy and personal struggles with depression. Jakes turned his life into his art and now shines as a complex tension between comforter and capitalist.

Jakes' early experiences were responsible for many of the postmodern characteristics that would later distinguish him. Growing up in a racially mixed environment and family setting that lacked religious indoctrination contributed to the doctrinal flexibility and racially generic message that characterize his current ministry. Jakes' early conflicts in a pious Christian community helped shape a highly spiritual yet profoundly human message that reverberates with people turned off by traditional religion. Jakes left the black Baptist tradition of his youth that emphasized God's grace and human frailty to join a Pentecostal experience where Christians emphasized power and holiness; and part of his future success would be to utilize both traditions of spiritual fervor and human frailty. Today Jakes transcends racial and denominational lines with a therapeutic approach to Christianity that addresses the existential concerns of many people.

Jakes' early preaching days also left indelible marks on his future message and ministry. These were the days when he preached in storefront churches throughout coal-mining towns, experienced abject poverty, and watched his wife give birth to most of his children. These were days in which Jakes had to thumb rides to church after his car was repossessed, and they were the days he relocated his ministry three times to expand his career. There were even those rough days when he felt like wrapping it all up. But Jakes conquered fear, depression, misfortune, and poverty, and people throughout West Virginia began to appreciate his distinctive message and ministry.

Jakes' ascent is the rags-to-riches story of an underdog making use of a once-in-a-lifetime opportunity to transcend anonymity. Jakes spent many years traveling and ministering alone, and in many ways he is a self-creation. But his individual hard work and ambition converged with the assistance from useful allies and systems already put into place by leaders of a neo-Pentecostal movement. Hence, it is impossible to explain Jakes' explosive rise to celebrity without mentioning the neo-Pentecostal media revolution that preceded his rapid emergence: Jakes is the product of specific conditions at a particular historical moment. Neo-Pentecostal television broadcast networks prepared a nondenominational route to fame that Oral Roberts, Jimmy Swaggart, Benny Hinn, Carlton Pearson, and Jakes would take through national television exposure. This ability to blur denominational lines is one of the postmodern features that distinguish neo-Pentecostalism and Jakes' ministry.

Though fortuitous events introduced Jakes to the world in the early 1990s, shrewd marketing, organizational savvy, and continued exposure on national television made him a superstar. Jakes was a quick study after receiving his big break at the AZUSA Conference, and the country preacher swiftly reinvented himself as a flashy high-tech neo-Pentecostal. Shortly after his rise in fame and finances, a media blitz of negative publicity concerning Jakes' new opulent lifestyle drove him out of West Virginia to his current environs in Dallas. Repositioning his budding ministry was a gutsy move that could have easily backfired. Jakes' conferences quickly began drawing tens of thousands of participants nationwide as he traversed the preaching/lecturing circuit and expanded his influence among politicians and celebrities. Jakes dramatically increased his market share through creative endeavors including music CDs, theatrical productions, a best-selling novel, and his own line of Hallmark cards, while traveling the country as a motivational speaker. By the end of 2004, Jakes was a pastor of a 28,000 member church appearing before millions four times a week on television; an author writing several best-selling books with a large secular publishing company; the executive producer of a movie; and an entrepreneur enjoying a first-class lifestyle.

Fred Price was an important pioneer of a prosperity message reflecting the values and tensions of the burgeoning wealth and consumption of the 1980s. Hence it is no coincidence that the rise of black word churches teaching prosperity theology occurred during the decade when the number of middle- and upper-class African Americans increased dramatically. Jakes co-opted the prosperity gospel early in his career and combined it with his own unique style of philosophical pragmatism to form a message that is compatible with a capitalistic society striving for success. Jakes' television broadcasts and books inspire many to believe that God wants all Christians to enjoy the good life.

Jakes' prosperity teaching allows him to boast freely about his lavish lifestyle as a sign of God's blessing. Prosperity preachers like Jakes embrace consumer culture and express little concern for the unequal distribution of wealth or challenging the ways our social structure relates to exploitation. Proponents of the liberationist perspective scowl at a perceived nexus of faith and finances and contend that Jakes promotes a bourgeois gospel that would not be effective in geopolitical contexts requiring a dramatic restructuring of society to make faith and individual agency relevant. Conversely, supporters claim that the civil rights age of protest is passé and that Jakes offers a new message of liberation by envisioning poor people with resources, power, and excelling in all areas through self-determination and faith.

Targeting sermons, books, and conferences to women fulfills the dual task of helping people in pain and expanding Jakes' market share. Considering his widespread influence over women, Jakes surprisingly has received little scrutiny from feminist theologians. Jakes is a feminist who exhorts women to dream big and have their shining moment in history. But Jakes also has an antifeminist side with his proclivity for objectifying women with repeated allusions to their anatomy and by depicting them as weaker vessels, caretakers of men, and coddlers of their husbands' fears and insecurities. Jakes' sympathy for women's issues while reinforcing essentialist notions of gender is part of the contradiction in his life and ministry.

Jakes' commercialized spirituality celebrates the hypercapitalist values of his age. He often defends his extraordinary wealth by reminding critics that he is both a businessman and a minister and that God has bountifully blessed both missions, but his followers are often naive about how the nexus of businessman and minister forms a strategic multimillion-dollar machine. Jakes the preacher offers spiritual wisdom and insight while Jakes the businessman is an aggressive entrepreneur exploring the most effective ways to market his spiritual gifts. A myopic view of Jakes as just a spiritual leader obscures the reality that much of his wealth comes from commercializing religion and that some of his decisions place the interests of the entrepreneurial empire above his integrity. He utilizes businesspersons, media moguls, and publicists to help him package and market religious commodities to maintain or increase his market share. Such pressure to standardize products for mass consumption may be causing a loss of prophetic edge.

An important aspect of Jakes' American features involves a willingness to market God in a language that many people can understand. An economic approach that studies churches as companies competing to offer religious products for potential clients is helpful in understanding Jakes' mass appeal. Such an approach assumes that forces of supply and demand influence religious choices as they do in commercial realms, and that religious suppliers seek to be unique along dimensions that are widely valued by clients. This new voluntarism reflects an understanding of religious participation that is based less on duty or obligation to inherited faiths and more on whether religious institutions meet people's needs. Jakes is both the product and producer of a segment of American popular religion that offers a more subjective, self-empowering, therapeutic spirituality that reverberates with contemporary Americans.

We have discussed the convergence of many postmodern features involved in constructing Jakes and American popular religion, but this should be qualified in the context of a relatively theologically conservative phenomenon. For example, the rapid decline of the AZUSA Fellowship and Carlton Pearson's influence because of his embrace of a controversial doctrine demonstrates an unrelenting intolerance of liberal theology. Similarly, Jakes' decision to hide his rejection of the Trinity in fear of losing his mainstream supporters exhibits doctrinal inflexibility atypical of postmodernism. Because they adhere to biblical authority and fully endorse the doctrinal tenets as orthodox Christianity, Jakes and his neo-Pentecostal peers are theologically conservative while being part of a contemporary-looking package.

But pastors like Jakes are still postmodern because they have multidimensional ministries that are drawing from pop culture, offering therapeutic religion, and utilizing commercial networks, technology, and mass media to transform their spiritual gifts into salable commodities. Neo-Pentecostals like Jakes are postmodern in the sense that they form a loosely organized movement that is blurring denominational lines of distinction and challenging traditional ways of seeing the world and religion. They are also postmodern because of their disdain for conventionality and for making spirituality practical rather than esoteric. The mixing of codes from religion with elements of contemporary and secular culture is at the heart of their distinctiveness.

An unrelenting respect for biblical authority has always been a feature of American popular religion. Jakes and many neo-Pentecostal preachers are widely accepted because they conform to cultural tastes and preferences while maintaining conservative theology. Currently there exists no thriving Protestant movement or denomination that does not affirm the historical reliability of scripture. Hence there is a difference between appreciating a postmodern packaging of the faith and accepting postmodern theological assumptions about truth, history, and authoritative knowledge. Jakes represents a conservative style of postmodernism in an evangelical American spiritual marketplace.

Discussing the spread of neo-Pentecostalism in terms of a revolution may unsettle those who frown at any form of parallelism between spiritual and political movements, but the two spheres share an intriguing similarity. Political revolutions come from a growing sense that existing institutions have failed to address the problems and needs of a society (Kuhn 1996). Similarly, throughout history, prophets provoked radical changes when the church disregarded the relevant needs of the masses. As with the Montanist reaction to Catholicism in the fourth century, Methodist and Baptist revivals of the nineteenth century, classical Pentecostalism of the twentieth century, and neo-Pentecostalism of today, spiritual revolutions occur when existing religious institutions lose their vitality and fail to be relevant to the human condition.

Neo-Pentecostalism is contemporary Christianity in its postmodern form and wages war against denominationalism, religiosity, and traditionalism. Like most bloody revolutions, neo-Pentecostalism produces many casualties in the form of dying mainline churches that cannot compete with the flexibility, ingenuity, and spiritual vitality exhibited by Jakes' postmodern approach to Christianity. Reminiscent of the mom-and-pop stores that lose customers to large grocery chains that offer an abundance of products, small neighborhood churches are finding it increasingly difficult to compete with mega churches that offer more choices under one roof. Those churches that adjust to a changing American worldview will flourish, while those that lag behind may lose many of their followers.

The decline of mainline denominations and the rise of postmodern spirituality demonstrate that religious institutions are challenged to integrate the tastes and preferences of their environs in order to remain relevant. As neo-Pentecostal mega churches continue to become powerful forces in American Protestantism, new standards will be established regarding conventional church culture. The standardized approach to praise and worship, gospel music, and technology in many black and white neo-Pentecostal churches already demonstrate the process of establishing a new "traditional" church experience.

But with most successful revolutions comes the threat of becoming institutionalized, and thus a counterrevolution is always lurking. As the postmodern mega church develops into the popular blueprint for success, it becomes a greater target for attacks by Christians who find fault with its flash and style, contemporary music, high-tech services, prosperity preaching, and mass marketing of spiritual commodities. Detractors may launch invasive attacks against the faith industry of media hype and commercialization that produces superstar preachers almost overnight. The ardent critics that Jakes' ministry generates are evidence that shock troops for the counterrevolution have already borne arms.

America and Jakes

Throughout the past centuries, scholars, journalists, and social commentators have attempted to capture America's essence. As one writer put it, America's brilliance comes from "a certain elasticity in our processes that allows us to change, adjust, and deal with the changing pressures and needs of modern life, while holding onto the vision of those who went before us" (Halberstam 2003:23). Other commentators have suggested that a strong embrace of capitalism, a penchant for self-invention and reinvention, rugged individualism, and an insatiable appetite for success are qualities bearing our nation's character. It is not surprising that Jakes' life, message, and ministry reflect these American traits.

Jakes' rags-to-riches story is a combustible mixture of talent, timing, and tenacity and embodies all that is incorporated in what philosopher Cornel West calls the prevailing Horatio Alger mystique, "The widespread hopes and dreams for social upward mobility . . . the values, outlooks, and lifestyles of achievement, careerism, leisurism, and consumerism that pervade American culture" (West 2003:887). Armed with the courage and creativity to venture outside the box of traditional Protestantism, Jakes is the small-town preacher who transcended obscurity to achieve a special level of greatness. Mounting a television ministry, starting a record label, producing music CDs, gospel plays, and a movie, launching yearly conferences in stadiums, accepting a $35 million mortgage on a new church building, all required the entrepreneurial courage and sense of industry that embody the American spirit. The tenacity and ingenuity it took for his grandmother to pay her way through college by washing clothes reflects the same frontier spirit that helped Jakes become a national celebrity.

Jakes shares interesting similarities with the first quintessential American, Benjamin Franklin. Like Franklin, Jakes displays America's unique style of philosophical pragmatism through a Protestant ethic divorced from heavy dogma. Like Franklin, Jakes preaches a self-empowering bourgeois message that inspires ordinary individuals to become extraordinary citizens. Like Franklin, Jakes is an ambitious entrepreneur, a writer, a philosopher, a statesman, an adviser to the president, a business strategist, a political thinker, and a cultural icon. And most importantly, like Franklin, Jakes personifies the values and tensions of his era.

Billy Graham and T.D. Jakes also have much in common as media masters who have utilized the technological advances of their era to reach millions. Both Graham and Jakes are archetypes of Americanized Christianity, but in different eras. Graham was the beacon of Americanized Christianity in its modern form using civil religion as a springboard for leading people into an evangelical style of Christianity (Fishwick 2002). Jakes is the symbol of Americanized Christianity in its postmodern form using cultural tools from popular religion (psychotherapy, pop culture, and self-empowerment) to lead many people to a neo-Pentecostal style of Christianity that may commandeer the future. Age and weariness have caused Graham to become less relevant in our sight-and-sound generation, and Jakes has taken the mantle and is running away with it.

Jakes' amazing rise and success are largely attributable to his affinity with our postmodern age of hypercapitalism and media hype. Jakes emerged during a time when spirituality is commonly converted into salable goods and purchased through complex distribution systems and multifaceted arrangements in cyberspace. Jakes quickly learned how to exploit commercial networks and inundate Christians with spiritual images on television, radio broadcasts, the Internet, and Christian magazines to generate his buzz. Like movie stars and athletes, Jakes is the product of a technological age of mass communication that turns celebrities into valuable commodities.

But hype and media exposure were not enough to secure Jakes' market share; he drew followers by addressing the needs and cultural tastes of many American Christians. Jakes' appeal comes from a message peppered in pop culture and American idealism and from compassionately addressing problems ignored by other preachers such as sexual abuse, addiction, and abandonment. Whether he is using psychological theories or folk wisdom, Jakes appropriates a broad range of cultural tools at his disposal to fulfill the Apostle Paul's mantra of being all things to all men and women. Jakes' trenchant diagnosis of the human condition fuels his clever use of the gospel to address the existential concerns of listeners. Jakes fights what he perceives as hypocrisy in the church and motivates Christians to be open and honest about their frailties, and his message of uplift to the underdog resonates with an untapped market of people abandoned by pretentious Protestant churches. Jakes blends a spiritual mission with a profoundly American message of uplift to provide supernatural hope to despondent hearts. Jakes' cultural repertoire for solving practical life problems concerning finances, weight loss, self-esteem, and other issues strikes chords with many contemporary Americans. Jakes is America's preacher because he speaks to his generation.

While mainliners struggle to adjust their ministries toward changing times, Jakes has won unprecedented popularity by offering a relevant message to contemporary Americans. But many

critics contend that Jakes' needs-based approach co-opts the
gospel with a narcissistic focus on the personal benefits of the faith
while neglecting the costs. In this way, Jakes resembles Harry
Emerson Fosdick, the legendary pastor of Riverside Church in
New York, who some consider to be the first postmodern
preacher of the twentieth century. Fosdick appeared on the cover
of *Time* magazine more than seventy-five years before Jakes and
became one of the nation's leading preachers. Like Jakes, Fosdick
preached riveting sermons on the airways, wrote books, and was a
gifted speaker using technology to further the aims of Christianity.
And not unlike Jakes, Fosdick received much praise and criticism
for using the resources of the gospel to address the contemporary
needs of many people in his day. Jakes is both admired and disparaged for his relevance to contemporary society, making his life,
message, and ministry appear profoundly American.

Jakes is the prototype of the new multidimensional pastors who
generate millions each year through the mass marketing of their
spiritual gifts. A proud proponent of capitalism, he believes that
all of his talents and spiritual gifts are fair game for commercialization. Jakes and many popular pastors are spiritual descendants
of frontier preachers who trounced the Puritanical form of Christianity that dominated early American life a few centuries ago.
America's fondness of frontier expansion led to the demise of the
Puritans' emphases on asceticism and self-sacrifice and left Protestantism susceptible to a spirituality that embodies barefaced materialism, idealism, and a strong sense of industry. Hence it is not
surprising that many Protestants like Jakes offer a style of Christianity in line with the principles and values of our free market society and utilize technology and commercial networks to build
large spiritual machines.

As a final word, the Tommy Jakes who preached revivals in
West Virginia coal-mining towns during the humble days before
his big break is very different from the reinvented T.D. Jakes who
emerged in the years that followed. Tommy Jakes was raw, country, and conventional; T.D. Jakes is high-tech, flashy and cosmo-

politan. Tommy Jakes wore bright colors and high-water pants; T.D. Jakes dons voguish apparel and Armani suits. Tommy Jakes was accessible; T.D. Jakes is untouchable. Tommy Jakes drove an old rusty Valiant; T.D. Jakes sports a Bentley. Tommy Jakes was obese; T.D. Jakes is trimmer and fitter. Tommy Jakes was grass-roots; T.D. Jakes dines with high society. Tommy Jakes reflects the American dream in its gleaming possibilities; T.D. Jakes mirrors an American dream tainted by materialism. But one thing that has not changed is that from the depth of his soul to the core of his experience, Thomas Dexter Jakes is an American phenomenon.

Bibliography

Anderson, Robert Mapes. 1979. *Vision of the Disinherited: The Making of American Pentecostalism*. New York and Oxford: Oxford University Press.

Baer, Hans. 1992. *African-American Religion in the Twentieth Century: Varieties of Protest and Accommodation*. Knoxville: University of Tennessee Press.

Cox, Harvey. 2001. *Fire from Heaven: The Rise of Pentecostal Spirituality and the Reshaping of Religion in the 21st Century*. New York and Cambridge, MA: Da Capo Press.

Daniels, David. 2001. "African-American Pentecostalism in the 20th Century." In *The Century of the Holy Spirit: 100 Years of Pentecostal and Charismatic Renewal*, ed. Vinson Synan, 265–291. Nashville: Thomas Nelson Publishers.

Douglas, Kelly Brown. 1994. *The Black Christ*. Maryknoll, NY: Orbis Books.

Fergen, Kenneth. 1991. *The Saturated Self: Dilemmas of Identity in Contemporary Life*. New York: Basic Books.

Finke, Roger. 1997. "The Illusion of Shifting Demand: Supply-Side Interpretations of American Religious History." In *Retelling U.S. Religious History*, ed. Thomas A. Tweed, 108–124. Berkeley: University of California Press.

Finke, Roger, and Rodney Stark. 1992. *The Churching of America, 1776–1990: Winners and Losers in Our Religious Economy*. New Brunswick, NJ: Rutgers University Press.

Fishwick, Marshall. 2002. *Popular Culture in a New Age*. New York: Haworth Press.

Fitzgerald, F. Scott. 1991. *The Great Gatsby*. New York: Macmillan.

Franklin, Robert. 1997. *Another Day's Journey: Black Churches Confronting the American Crisis*. Minneapolis: Fortress.

Gilkes, Cheryl Townsend. 2001. *If It Wasn't for the Women: Black Women's Experience and Womanist Culture in Church and Community*. Maryknoll, NY: Orbis Books.

Grant, Jacquelyn. 1979. "Black Theology and the Black Woman." In *Black Theology: A Documentary History, 1966–1979*, ed. Gayraud S. Wilmore and James Cone, 418–432. Maryknoll, NY: Orbis Books.

Gregorian, Vartan. 2003. "The Promise of America." In *Defining a Nation: Our America and the Source of Its Strength*, ed. David Halberstam, 27–35. Washington, D.C.: National Geographic.

Halberstam, David. 2003. "Introduction." In *Defining a Nation: Our America and the Source of Its Strength*, ed. David Halberstam, 13–23. Washington, D.C.: National Geographic.

Harrison, Milmon. 2005. *Righteous Riches: The Word of Faith Movement in Contemporary African American Religion*. New York: Oxford University Press.

Hopkins, Dwight. 2003. "Slave Theology in the Invisible Institution." In *African American Religious Thought: An Anthology*, ed. Cornel West and Eddie Glaude Jr., 790–830. Louisville, KY: Westminster John Knox Press.

Jakes, Jacqueline. 2002. *Sister Wit: Devotions for Women*. New York: Warner Books.

Jakes, Serita Ann. 1999. *The Princess Within: Restoring the Soul of a Woman*. Minneapolis: Bethany House.

Jakes, T.D. 1994a. *Why? Because You Are Anointed*. Lanham, MD: Pneuma Life Publishing.

———. 1994b. *Can You Stand to Be Blessed: Insights to Help You Survive the Peaks and Valleys*. Shippensburg, PA: Destiny Image.

———. 1995. *Help Me I've Fallen and I Can't Get Up!* Dallas: T.D. Jakes.

———. 1996a. *Daddy Loves His Girls*. Orlando: Creation House.

———. 1996b. *The Harvest*. Lanham, MD: Pneuma Life Publishing.

———. 1996c. *Help! I'm Raising My Children Alone*. Lake Mary, FL: Charisma House.

———. 1997[1993]. *Woman, Thou Art Loosed: Healing the Wounds of the Past*. Shippensburg, PA: Destiny Image.

———. 1997a. *So You Call Yourself a Man? A Devotional for Ordinary Men with Extraordinary Potential*. Tulsa, OK: Albury Press.

———. 1997b. *Anointing Fall on Me: Assessing the Power of the Holy Spirit*. Lanham, MD: Pneuma Life Publishing.

———. 1998. *The Lady, Her Lover, and Her Lord*. New York: Berkley Books.

———. 1999. *Maximize the Moment: God's Action Plan for Your Life*. New York: G.P. Putnam's Sons.

———. 2000. *The Great Investment: Faith, Family and Finance*. New York: G.P. Putnam's Sons.

———. 2001[1995]. *Naked and Not Ashamed: We've Been Afraid to Reveal What God Longs to Heal*. Shippensburg, PA: Destiny Image.

———. 2002. *God's Leading Lady: Out of the Shadows and into the Light*. New York: G.P. Putnam's Sons.

———. 2003a. *Cover Girls: A Novel*. New York: Warner Faith.

———. 2003b. *Follow the Star: Christmas Stories That Changed My Life*. New York: G.P. Putnam's Sons.

Kuhn, Thomas. 1996. *The Structure of Scientific Revolutions*. Chicago: University of Chicago Press.

Lewter, Andy C. 1994. *Management Manual for the Full Gospel Baptist Church Fellowship*. Ministerial project for the Doctor of Ministry Program, United Theological Seminary.

Lincoln, C. Eric, and Lawrence Mamiya. 1990. *The Black Church in the African American Experience*. Durham, NC: Duke University.

Martin, David. 2002. *Pentecostalism: The World, Their Parish*. Malden, MA: Blackwell.

McRoberts, Omar M. 2003. *Streets of Glory: Church and Community in a Black Urban Neighborhood*. Chicago: University of Chicago Press.

Miller, Donald E. 1997. *Reinventing American Protestantism: Christianity in the New Millennium*. Berkeley: University of California Press.

Morris, Aldon, and Shayne Lee. 2005. "The National Baptist Convention: Tradition and the Challenges of Modernity." In *Church, Identity, and Change: Theology and Denominational Structures in Unsettled Times*. New York: Eerdmans.

Morton, Paul. 1999. *Why Kingdoms Fall: The Journey from Breakdown to Restoration*. Tulsa, OK: Albury.

Porter, Michael E. 1985. *Competitive Advantage: Creating and Sustaining Superior Performance*. New York: Free Press.

Roof, Wade Clark. 1999. *Spiritual Marketplace: Baby Boomers and the Remaking of American Religion*. Princeton, NJ: Princeton University Press.

Roof, Wade Clark, and William McKinney. 1987. *Mainline American Religion: Its Changing Shape and Future*. New Brunswick, NJ: Rutgers University Press.

Rosenau, Pauline Marie. 1992. *Post-Modernism and the Social Sciences: Insights, Inroads, and Intrusions*. Princeton, NJ: Princeton University Press.

Sargeant, Kimon Howland. 2000. *Promoting Traditional Religion in a Nontraditional Way*. New Brunswick, NJ: Rutgers University Press.

Stark, Rodney, and Roger Finke. 2000. *Acts of Faith: Explaining the Human Side of Religion*. Berkeley: University of California Press.

Starling, Kelly. 2001. "Why People, Especially Black Women, Are Talking about Bishop T.D. Jakes." *Ebony*, January.

Tweed, Thomas A. 1997. "Introduction: Narrating U.S. Religious History." In *Retelling U.S. Religious History*, ed. Thomas A. Tweed, 1–23. Berkeley: University of California Press.

West, Cornel. 2003. "Black Theology and Marxist Thought." In *African American*

Religious Thought: An Anthology, ed. Cornel West and Eddie Glaude Jr., 874–893. Louisville, KY: Westminster John Knox Press.

Wilmore, Gayraud S. 1998. *Black Religion and Black Radicalism: An Interpretation of the Religious History of African Americans.* Maryknoll, NY: Orbis Books.

Wuthnow, Robert. 1988. *The Restructuring of American Religion.* Princeton, NJ: Princeton University Press.

Index

About the Author

Professor Shayne Lee earned a Ph.D. in sociology at Northwestern University and is currently Assistant Professor of Sociology and African Diaspora Studies at Tulane University. Professor Lee studies contemporary cultural changes in African American churches and teaches courses on culture, race and ethnicity, postmodern society, mass communication, and African American religion.